WOMEN'S RIGHTS IN INDIA

A Feminist Perspective

WOMEN'S RIGHTS IN INDIA

A Feminist Perspective

By

Dr. Rekha Roy

AKANSHA PUBLISHING HOUSE

NEW DELHI - 110 002 (INDIA)

AKANSHA PUBLISHING HOUSE
4649-B/21, Ansari Road
Darya Ganj, New Delhi - 110 002
Ph.: 23263193/9811582579
Fax: 011-23263193
Email: ektabooks@yahoo.com

Women's Rights in India: A Feminist Perspective

First Published 2006
ISBN 81-8370-093-4

[The responsibility for the facts stated, conclusions reached etc., is entirely that of the Authors. The publisher is not responsible for them, whatsoever.]

PRINTED IN INDIA

Published by M.P. Misra for Akansha Publishing House, New Delhi and Printed at Aryan Enterprises, Delhi

Dedication

To my son Parash

Contents

Foreword

Feminism is an ideological movement that transformed the way life is lived in most societies across the globe because societies, excepting a few of them, had taken to a patriarchal social, cultural, familial and personal life-style since long. Being ideological, feminism is also a philosophical movement and the interest of philosophers in feminist ideologies has been pronounced, especially in recent times. Of course, feminism is also activism but activism based primarily in a meticulously worked out ideology. One approach to the feminist argument is heavily loaded with biological and physical analogies and claims made rather scientifically that nature has not actually made the sexual division of labour on strictly polarized lines as has been claimed so often by patriarchal ideologies. Another approach to the same argument is based not so much on biological comparisons of the sexes but on the principle of equality of all human beings as humans and takes a human rights approach to the feminist perspective. This second approach has been increasingly gaining ground in the twentieth century and thenceforth. Here gender-based division of labour, gender-based social taboos, the infamous unfreedoms of women, the objectification of the woman's womanhood, the painting of women as soft and fragile and breakable are all perceived as a definite masculine agenda which can be redrawn, demystified, deconstructed and freed from the obvious bias on the basis of the principle of equality and the inherent humanity of women.

In her book, *Women's Right in India*, Dr. Rekha Roy has taken this second stance and offers some probing analysis of the history, philosophy and cultural constructions that bind together the Indian image of woman. Although in a typically patriarchal fashion women were allowed certain freedom and respect in the Vedic times, this situation progressively regressed. In Manu's law book women are painted as those needing not only protection and care but also those who are to be carefully guarded and restrained for the unchallenged progress of man. During the British times situation had reached the 'dark age' mark when women were burned with her husband's corpse, women were married off as children, women were mostly disallowed personal property and largely debarred from social interaction and a life of self-actualization. The situation has only improved slowly since the birth of modern India and Independence. Rights of women are still not perceived as such by the society due to generations of cultural conditioning. *Women's Rights in India* looks into all these aspects and clarifies important concepts like rights, humans rights, women's rights etc., and their rationale. The author does not stop at that but goes on to suggest what measures and social steps can really allow women to claim and accept their rights.

I zealously recommend Dr. Rekha Roy's work to a wide readership. It will make for interesting reading to feminists, activists, philosophers, teachers and students of women's studies and to the general readers as the book is written lucidly and with as little academic niceties as possible.

Shillong
July 2006

JAGAT PAL
Professor & Head, Deptt. of Philosophy North-Eastern Hill University, Shillong

Acknowledgements

"Women's Rights in India: A Feminist Perspective" is a revised version of the Ph.D dissertation I submitted to the North Eastern Hill University in 2004. Living among the matrilineal Khasi tribe of Meghalaya, I was intriguingly drawn to compare the situation of Khasi women and that of the vast majority of Indian women. That is how this research topic came to be decided upon. I realize that it was a worthwhile project, which has enriched me a thousand fold.

As such, I am extremely grateful to all who helped me complete the research and prepare the final output for publication. My special debt of gratitude goes to Prof. Jagat Pal, now Head of the Department of Philosophy, NEHU, who supervised my research and wrote the foreword to this book. I thank him for his various suggestions, guidance and the interest he showed in my work. I also would like to thank the other teachers and non-teaching staff of the Department for their help, discussions and timely support. A special word of thanks goes to Prof. Sujata Miri, earlier Dean of the Schcol of Humanities and Education, NEHU, for her advice and warm support. I am grateful to Dr. Gurudas Das, Head, Department of Humanities and Social Sciences, National Institute of Technology, Silchar for taking a special interest in seeing my work published.

I am deeply indebted to my husband, Mr. Pranesh Roy, who constantly and affectionately prodded me to complete the work up to the stage of preparing this manuscript for publication. I also would like to acknowledge my little son Master Parash, who unhappily missed his mother a great deal when I was busily involved in research. My mother and father, Mrs. G. Ojha and Mr. B. N. Ojha, helped me complete this work in every possible way. I am deeply indebted to them. Dr. Siby K. George, Lecturer, HSS Department, NIT Silchar, who proofread this manuscript and made suggestions for its improvement before sending it to the press, and the Akansha Publishing House, New Delhi, my publishers, deserve a special note of thanks. In this acknowledgement, if I have inadvertently missed out the names of friends who contributed to this work in any way, apologies and thanks to them all.

Shillong, 2006 **Dr. Rekha Roy**

1

Introduction

This book is an attempt to analyze and examine some of the social and moral issues pertaining to the rights of women in India, which are widely debated in contemporary Indian society among pro and anti feminists.

All social and moral issues pertaining to the rights of women are conceptually connected to the notion of 'human rights.' The rights of women, of children, of disabled people, of migrants and refugees and of people belonging to less privileged classes and minorities are not outside the domain of human rights but rather fall within it. So, any examination of social and moral issues pertaining to the rights of women presupposes first an analysis of the concept of human rights itself because all women's rights come within the domain of human rights.

Human rights are generally defined in philosophical literature as those rights which are inherent in our nature and without which we cannot live as dignified human beings. The addition of the adjective 'human' to the term 'right' signifies that every person (every 'human' being) is entitled to them. Human rights do not belong to any particular society, community or person, but to the community of humankind as a whole. There is a debate about whether all members of human race have equal claim to these rights or whether some persons such as infants, children and the insane persons deserve relatively more rights than others. There is also a debate whether groups can claim human rights in the same sense as individual human persons. If the basic qualification for having human rights is to belong to the human race as a born-equal, then all humans have equal human rights, irrespective of age, sex, culture and such other differences. This follows from the very concept of humanity itself. This natural moral claim is articulated and formulated in what we today call 'human rights'. In fact, there is a huge international movement for the preservation of human rights and international, national and other smaller human rights groups exist to claim these rights for individuals and groups who are in the gravest danger of being denied them. All other rights such as economic rights, political rights and legal rights are ultimately justified by referring to the concept of human natural rights which are considered to be the most basic and fundamental rights of human beings.

The nature of human rights does not make them a vague set of desires and needs. As with every right, in the legal sense of the term, human right is also characterized by its subject, i.e., the holder of the right, a specific object and a guarantee. In the case of human rights, the subjects or holders of rights are the whole human race, i.e., men, women and children irrespective of sex, religion, ethnicity, geographical origin, age etc. The object of law is specified and stated in internationally recognized texts or in the national law. For example, education, freedom of expression, freedom of thought, nationality and culture are given in the declarations and conventions and covenants drawn up by international bodies. Every right is enforceable against third parties that may not respect it. The right of appeal is guaranteed. In the case of human rights, guarantees are afforded primarily by the international institutions when they are translated into law by the law creating authorities of various countries. But they should also be ensured by all the institutions responsible for people's everyday lives (state, regional institutions, specialized institutions, ministries etc.) and by each individual as a responsible human being.

Surely, we cannot demand for a whole series of unrestricted freedom and say endlessly 'I am entitled to ....', without respecting other people as much as ourselves and without recognizing that they have the same rights. No one can decide certain human rights as more important than others. Human rights form a whole and represent a set of values and principles that all human beings in all countries and in all cultures are morally bound to respect. All individuals should strive to realize for themselves and for others, the full range of human rights.

The concept of human rights has gradually evolved over the past several centuries. It is immaterial whether one calls these rights as inherent rights, fundamental rights or by some other name. These rights by themselves have no fixed content and most of them are empty vessels into which each generation has poured its contents in the light of its experience. Human rights, as conceived in the last few decades of the twentieth century, are morally justified claims because they preserve and promote human goodness. They are owned by individuals, by states as well as by the organized social and economic groups morally. Morality is the centre of power and authority. Human rights are believed to have existed in however nascent a form ever since human beings as gregarious animals have lived in communities, families, clans, tribes, villages, towns, nations or now in an independent world community.

Any viable conception of human rights, which can be acceptable to the modern liberal democratic societies, must fulfill at least two basic conditions. First, the rights must be equal and effective. Second, there must be an obligation on others to accept the rights. Hobbesian and Lockian views of natural human rights do not meet these requirements. The inability of both these views to meet this requirement is due to their basic postulates, which make it impossible to produce a new acceptable theory of human rights. Both writers imputed to the nature of society a permanent conflict of interest between individuals. Hobbes' men necessarily sought power over others. Locke's national men sought unlimited property, which he assumed, must be at the expense of others. Thus classical liberalism, which lies at the heart of the natural tradition, cannot be acceptable to modern liberal democratic societies as it rests on the sanctification of bourgeois self-interests. The Hobbesian and Lockian concept of natural rights is not acceptable now and no extension of them can be made generally acceptable because of their possessive individualist postulates. Although these conceptions of natural rights were supposed to express the human essence, and were claimed in the name of human freedom, but now these are not regarded as a sufficient statement of human essence or freedom, even in the countries where they originated. The liberal democratic concept of human rights in the second half of the twentieth century has come to mean defence of the rights of human beings against abuse of power committed by the organs of the state with the help of institutionalized means. It also involves the promotion of establishment of human living conditions and overall development of the human personality as a whole.

If we are to assess the central claims of the natural rights tradition, we need a better understanding of them. We must know what makes a right a natural right. If humanity constitutes the ground of natural human rights, we must first know what constitutes humanity. When we go through the writings on natural human rights, unfortunately we do not find a satisfactory answer to this question. The existence of natural rights has been affirmed both in political rhetoric and political theory. Rhetorical assertion of such rights has usually taken the form of declarations or manifestos in the service of some political cause. These documents are not remembered chiefly for the depth of their philosophical reflection. Declarations and manifestos seldom offer grounding for their catalogues of rights and they never offer an account of what makes a right a natural right.

Moral rights are derived by the natural rights theorists from the concept of humanity. They are not considered conventional rights. Conventional rights are considered the products of human-made rule systems of some sort or other. In this sense conventional rights are different from natural human rights. Since conventional rules confer only conventional rights, the rules needed to confer natural moral rights cannot be conventional. Natural moral rights rest on a *priori* rational principles. Constitutional and legal rights are conventional rights because these rights are accorded by the will of a legislator. In other words, natural moral rights are inborn rights while the constitutional and legal rights are human determined rights. Natural moral rights belong to everyone. They are independent of all juridical acts of experience. Legal rights rest on the juridical acts. But natural rights do not rest on juridical acts. They are derived from the concept of humanity. But the idea of 'humanity' or 'a state of nature' is a very vague idea on which the natural rights theorists do not agree.

Thus, human rights are considered to be of two kinds: natural and conventional. Right to liberty, right to equality, right to dignity, right to life, right to fulfill needs and aspirations, right to defence and protection, right to enjoyment etc., are considered natural human rights which belong to both men and women. Right to productivity, right to abortion etc., are women's specific natural rights because these rights belong to women only and not to men. Right to education, right to property, right to equal pay for equal work, right to employment, legal rights, economic, social, cultural and religious rights are considered non-natural human or conventional rights because these rights are accorded on women and men by the human society. Between these two different kinds of rights, the natural moral rights are more fundamental. Conventional rights in fact are derived from and are justified by referring to natural moral rights. Conventional rights are specific rights; they differ from society to society and nation to nation. Women's conventional rights are specific rights because they differ from context to context, society to society and nation to nation. Women's natural rights are universal rights; they are not conditioned by the specificities of race, caste, colour, religion and situation. Thus any analysis and examination of the social and moral issues pertaining to women's rights always requires an analysis and examination of both natural and conventional rights which we cannot do without analyzing the concept of right itself since they logically rest on the latter.

The concept of right has been analysed and viewed by different philosophers in different ways by adopting different criteria of rights. According to some philosophers the concept of right is essentially linked with the concept of duty. For them the notion of 'right' and the notion of 'duty' or 'obligation' are correlative. But some philosophers do not subscribe to this view. According to them 'rights' and 'duties' are not correlative because there can be rights without duties. But whatever the case might be, in the context of women's rights, I have argued that rights and duties are correlative because women and men are capable of recognizing autonomy in others and of full participation in the moral community. But to say this does not mean that only such is the quality for the possession of rights. The notion of 'women's rights' involves in it the notion of power, privileges and claims but at the same time it also imposes duty on others to recognize women's autonomy. Defenders of women's rights, that is, feminists, are often unclear about this in their mind. If women have rights, then others are deemed to have duty to respect their rights, which means either to refrain from interfering with their free exercise of their rights or to assist women in attaining their rights, as the case may be and as the circumstances require and permit. Normally basic moral rights cannot be forfeited, compromised or overridden by the acts of others or even of ourselves but in certain circumstances there are exceptions. To say that women have certain natural moral rights is not to say that their natural moral rights are absolute, inalienable or indefensible. I have argued that traditional natural rights theorists' account cannot be defended because under exceptional conditions certain natural moral rights justifiably may be abrogated. Conflicts between individuals are common in society and moral principles and institutions have to be evolved to deal with them in ways that are fair to those concerned. If in accordance with law a woman labourer upon the performance of labour has a right to the wages for which she was contracted, she can legitimately claim the sum agreed upon and that it is the legal duty of the employer to satisfy this claim by paying the wage; if a woman has a legal right to the exclusive enjoyment of a certain piece of property, she can lawfully claim immunity from any interference on the part of others for her exclusive enjoyment of that piece of property, and that it is the legal duty of those others to refrain from such interference. But this is possible only when we assume that positive laws give rise to positive legal rights and correlated duties.

The feminists raise the question about women's rights because women's rights have been violated since the beginning of human civilization. They have been violated not because women are physically and mentally weak but because of the fact that social structures framed by men and because of their attitudes towards women. To say this does not mean that men's rights were not violated. History evidences that some categories of men were also deprived from the exercise of their rights. But that is a different aspect to the study of rights which I have not addressed in this book as it falls outside its scope. In any discussion of women's rights, we should not forget that all women do not face the same kind of problems. They face different kinds of problems because of their different socio-cultural and geographical conditions. Even within Indian society the status of all women is not the same. It differs from context to context and hence requires special consideration or preferential treatment in order to improve their lives. There may be a lot of debate on the question of preferential treatment of women. But I have argued that preferential treatment for women is not morally unjustified because its aim is to level the playing field, to provide genuine equality of opportunity. Equality in all respect may not be possible, nonetheless equality of opportunity is desirable and to avail this, the playing field must be equal. Discrimination is an unjust denial of equal treatment. But preferential treatment for women does not involve discrimination because it is a programme to promote equality of opportunity for women who have been and continue to be the victims of men's systematic discrimination. Women's rights are not only violated by men but also are violated by women themselves. History of Indian society is full of evidences for this.

Many questions may be raised about the rights of women such as what rights do they have? Who has accorded rights to them? What does it mean to say that women possess certain rights in virtue of humanity and womanhood? Are there women's natural rights? What constitutes humanity and womanhood? Natural rights feminists believe that women possess human rights in virtue of their nature, i.e., humanity and womanhood. Theological rights feminist believe that women's rights are accorded to them by God. Other feminists believe that no ground can be given for possession of women's rights, because it is self-evident that all humans, men and women, have certain basic moral rights which at any cost should be preserved and promoted for the wellbeing of men and women of any society or culture. Because of these and other difficulties with the notion of rights, many anti-feminists have argued that talk of women's rights have no value in moral theory and hence should be avoided altogether in our discussion of moral issues. I have argued that the basic moral rights, no matter where from they are derived, lie at the core of our system of moral beliefs and are essential for the development of individuals and society as a whole. All feminists no doubt believe that women have certain basic moral rights which have been violated by men and the society since the beginning of human civilization, but disagree about the nature of and solution to the subordination of women. They agree that women's oppression, exploitation and subordination exist in all the societies, which are morally wrong and hence must be eliminated. Right to equality, right to freedom of speech and participation in meetings, decisions, comparable pay for comparable work and income production, are considered women's issues in general. Special issues pertaining to women's rights depend largely on particular contexts but in certain cases conceptual understanding is required.

The conceptual understanding of the social and moral issues pertaining to women's rights contributes to a large extent in solving the problem of women's rights. Conceptual moorings of feminism have not been addressed often seriously by feminists themselves. I have tried to address myself to some of the conceptual issues in order to examine the debate between pro and anti feminists pertaining to women's rights.

The women's liberation or Feminist Movement of 1960s conceptualized women's problems as rooted in sexism. Sexism means women as a group is oppressed, subjugated in male defined and male structured social institutions and value systems. It assumes 'natural superiority of man' which was manifested as the power of men over women. It is the biological phenomena of sexism, which some of the feminists thought, is the prime cause of women's oppression, exploitation and domination by men through the ages. I have argued that the ideological foundations of sexism lies in the male culture that assumes inferiority of women. And this male culture is reflected in all social institutions, namely, the distribution of work, rewards and power in the family, in religion and culture. Interestingly, many social institutions, such as education, legal systems, marriage and nuclear family with their supportive myths perpetuated the male culture. The idea and social institutions combine in one to tie women to their dependent role as mother, daughter, wife and housekeeper. These issues I have highlighted in detail in the Second Chapter of the book. Besides, I have also tried to throw some light on the theoretical perspective and methodological orientations, specific to gender studies.

History of human civilization shows that women have been deprived and continues to be deprived of their rights throughout ages. It is a bitter truth that Indian women have not yet come out of the shackles of the 'womanhood attire' imposed successfully on them by men. Gender biased laws are still an unavoidable fact. Though women are quite capable of dealing with the normal situation, they are raped by criminals. But that does not invalidate this argument since a man can also be killed or badly mauled by a lunatic. These are the highlights of the discussions of the Third Chapter of the book.

In Chapter Four, I discuss about women's rights, which feminists classify as general and specific in kind. In this chapter I also discuss about the concept of rights, human rights, natural rights, women's rights and the rights of women in this country. It is a matter of fact that there exists mistreatment, subordination, oppression and exploitation of women in various forms in every society including the Indian one, which results from not protecting and preserving women's basic human rights. I have discussed the whole pyramid of violations of women's rights and their rationale in Chapter Five. In order to safeguard the wellbeing of Indian women, the protection and promotion of their rights ought to be done by the individuals, institutions and society because they still remain even today slaves with no identity. Men folk will have to share collective responsibility for the upliftment of women because unflinching male chauvinism has been responsible for this existing condition of women. Women deserve preferential treatment or special consideration on this count. I have discussed in detail issues and the conceptual framework regarding the protection of the rights of women. The themes emerging from the analysis of women's rights and issues pertaining to it have been summarized in the Conclusion.

2

Theories of Feminism

Feminist theory and gender studies have become significant cognitive enterprises in the last few decades. The societal-existential basis for the emergence and development of this branch of knowledge necessitates rigorous intellectual analysis within the paradigm of the sociology of knowledge. The fact that gender studies are not restricted by narrow boundaries of specific disciplines signifies the cognitive concerns which are interdisciplinary and cross-disciplinary, encompassing diverse theoretical orientations and perspectives within its explanatory framework.

It is important to make a conceptual distinction between femaleness, feminity and feminism. Femaleness is the physical and biological distinction between man and woman. Such a differentiation is chromosomically shaped and is part of the commonality of all living species. The reproductive organs are basically different at birth. With physical growth, the level of average height, weight, size of the body, quality of voice etc., become the characteristic features of gender distinctions. Feminity is the social, cultural and psychological transformation of gender as a distinctive category bearing philosophical meaning. Such a construction is made possible through institutionalized internalization of value, standardization of norms, typification of roles, structures of patriarchal styles of life, formation of customs like dowry, widowhood, unwed motherhood, duality of moral standards, emphasis on virginity, fidelity, religious rituals, notion of purity and pollution and attitudes of preferences and prejudices for and against one gender or another. Feminism is an ideological position which aims at structural and cultural transformation for equality of opportunity for women and elimination of all social forces which lead to discrimination, oppression and exploitation of women in visible or invisible, open or hidden, overt or covert processes and patterns. It has developed through women's movements and has articulated women's voices in cognitive-theoretical ways and activist-transformative forms for status equality in a gender-wise divisive world and worldview.

The question of theoretical perspectives and methodological orientations, specific to gender studies, are characterized by cognitive pluralism. However, an issue, which is philosophically problematic, which involves emotive sensitivity, which concerns half the human beings, which is a major focus for committed activists, governments and international organizations, and which has diverse theoretical positions, instead of enrichment, turns into epithets to condemn opponents.

Feminism, as an ideology, has several theoretical positions. As an ideology, the focus of feminism is empowerment of women, their emancipation, creation of equality, elimination of oppression and discrimination. Ethno-feminism focuses on structural and cultural specificities of regional and local levels, and emphasizes on the need for different forms of emancipation which are contextual. Ethno-feminism attempts coalition of differentiations rather than oppositional divisiveness. Difference ought not to become a point of immobility but solidarity.[1]

Feminism as a discursive practice focuses on the ways in which theory and practice interact mutually.[2] As an emanicipatory project, feminism has borrowed from the traditional Marxist position to cover its political and intellectual goals, thus fusing theory with practice. Women traditionally accepted the reality of their situation through the structure of patriarchy, emotive and binding force of familial love, distinctive cultural patterns and styles of life and value systems. The power, dominance and hegemony were subtly built into the institutions and modes of interpersonal relationship between men and women. Thus the male hegemony got its legitimacy through the willing and recognized consent of the oppressed and discriminated women.

There are various ways to categorize feminist theories. The basis of each categorization is different. From one perspective, the categorization is as follows:[3]

Feminist theory is a self-conscious reaction to overwhelming masculinity of privileged and historically dominant knowledge. The academic and cognitive constructions are located in a man's world of experience in accordance with his experience of reality and his definition of the problematic. The medium of thinking, language, itself favours one mode of thinking and communication. Meanings of the words are derived from the structure of language. Saussure theorized language as an abstract system having several signs. Each sign is made up of a signifier (sound or written image) and a signified (meaning). There is no intrinsic relation between the 'word' and the 'object'. It is an arbitrary naming game. Every word gets its meaning in articulation. Language thus structures our ideologies.

The vocabulary of everyday life creates meaning at the level of objective expression and indexical expression, which exemplify asymmetrical male-female relationship. 'He' and 'she' have social meaning and people perceive, anticipate and act accordingly.

The focus of the conventional theory of stratification has been class, caste and race but not gender. 'Status' of a male category is patriarchy. The mindsets tend to be gender based. Male preferences determine what is to be written and how it has to be described and interpreted. Functionalism by implication justifies *status quo*, and therefore it justifies also gender status quo. Females make more adjustment and are socialized to do so. Thereby they make the system cohesive and integrative. The interactionists have neglected the gender-power relation in the interactional processes. Social scientists have not examined how women are socialized for weakness, dependency and also fear of success. Exchange theory has neglected the question of asymmetry in gender relationship. Conflict theorists have focused on class analysis and have neglected 'gender.'

The institutional and academic structure of educational institutions perpetuates and intensifies the empirical reality by converting it into a cognitive form. School textbooks typify roles, do not mention contribution of women and use vocabulary and language which satisfy men. In universities there are courses and streams which are typified as male and female, like home science for girls and mathematics for boys, engineering for boys and medicine for girls. The syllabus and course contents are very insensitive to the issues of women. Mostly men formulate and design these courses. In seminars and orientation courses it is not uncommon to observe that male participants consider women as inferior and as ones who are meant for doing domestic roles. This is justified on the ground of women's physical condition. Women are considered physically weak. This argument is both naïve and archaic as the man-made culture does not emphasize horse power or elephant strength as important attributes of being human.

The methodological issues in feminism have several significant dimensions. Methodological femino-centrism focuses on the theme of gender-centredness, both in terms of issues and studies by females. Gender is one of the significant ascribed personal characteristics which influences the course of field work. It potentially influences access to the field, the collection of data and the interpretation of findings.

Gender identity, placement, visibility and expressiveness influence the processual dimension of data collection. The mode of interaction is different, and so is the nature and quality of dialoguing with the respondents. Gradually, the female researcher through experience and self-reflexivity challenges the andocentric assumptions of social life. The assumptions became the object of inquiry and help in establishing linkage between substantive theoretical issues and methodological interpretative issues. The process of growing up as a woman influences the mode and nature of understanding. This necessitates a process of academic de-socialization so that one discerns the self as different from standards set by men. Besides, there are sensitive and committed female researchers who have acquired the capacity to perceive the reality as man-made and the 'why' and 'how' of it. The experiential knowledge, which is part of women's existence, helps her to make a comprehensive analysis of gender situation by drawing on her experiential input. Her worldview is thus superimposed and juxtaposed with those who are like her. The scholar and woman thus became one without contradiction and dualism. This is necessary for those who want to do work 'for' women and not 'on' women.

Women field workers do not get entry into all situations on account of cultural reasons. However, it is sometimes easier for a western woman. There is a colonial hangover in certain sense. Men, often in a patriarchy, like to talk themselves as they consider it their privilege as head of the family to communicate and be a spokesperson of all in the family. Women live in a 'culture of silence.' However, conversation in a local dialect is of great importance in terms of establishing rapport and proper understanding for the field worker. The mobility of female researcher to remote places has its own constraints. Traveling alone, living alone and moving alone are part of unfamiliarity in many parts of India.

Understanding of women at certain levels of depth necessitates the use of biographical and case study methods. The biographical account of women should be analyzed to understand the institutional, structural and cultural sources of her life – what it has been as is! It is the qualitative dimension which reveals the layers of suppression, pathos, suffering, inequality, deprivation and discrimination. Biographical accounts help in unearthing the forces, factors, values, structures and practices which subordinate, typify and dis-empower women as a social category.

Representation of women in oral and living traditions, pictures, paintings, literature, religion, rituals, art forms, sculptures, architecture, media, pattern of houses, design of kitchen, their dresses, cosmetics, hair styles, manners, etiquettes norms, role expectations, value systems –especially sexual morality and double standards– can be investigated through context analysis, ideal-typical construction and comparative methods.

The activist orientation in feminist theory is a response to political aims and objectives of feminist struggle which is part of action programmes and activities. Praxis is the focus for the activists. The women activists have taken up significant issues from local-contextual to national-general levels. Activists have created organizations for providing employment to women. Women's organizations have taken up the issues of rape, dowry, bride burning, *sati*, prostitution and similar categories. Women's organizations have focused on both the specific and general issues of women. There are NGOs working in remote rural and tribal areas and also those located in urban centres.

The reflexive orientation sees theory through the theorist, action through the actor and discards the dichotomy between verbalized statements and personal action. It raises issues of morality and personal ethics. It is against institutionalized hypocrisy. Feminism is neither a fashion nor a fad. It necessitates serious involvement, opposition and if necessary, revolt against all those institutions, ideas, ideologies and idioms which suppress, suffocate, subordinate and make women suffer.

The cognitivistic interpretative feminist theory provides a framework based on gender (female) as a theoretical scheme for the analysis of society in its generality as well as its components. It takes into account feminist perspective for the analysis of power, inequality, family, religion and existential basis of knowledge. The history of human society is the history of female disempowerment in all structures and situations. Women as a universal category cuts across class, race, age, nationality, the entirety of society both at macro and micro levels and can be understood only through the women's perspective.

There are basically two types of versions in the feminist theory: (a) feminism of equality and (b) feminism of difference. The feminism of equality believes in the equality between genders and regards both human species as capable of achieving goals which the other can. The inequality is basically due to patriarchy which has domesticated, enslaved and sexualized women. Patriarchy dis-empowers women, typifies their roles and makes them dependent on men. The potentials of women have been curbed. They have been made to create a self-image as an object of beauty for the joy and enjoyment of men. The feminists of difference, on the other hand, emphasize the difference between men and women as the basis of essentialism, which is determined through biologism, naturalism and universalism. In biologism, women's essence is defined in terms of their biological capacities. This is a form of reductionism. In naturalism the feminism essentiality is traced on ontological and theological grounds. In universalism, the essence of women is contracted through universality of certain traits of women, found in all cultures. They reject the principles on which equality is measured. It believes in equality through differences. It objects to criterion of equality which takes male achievements, values and standards as the norms to which women should also aspire. It is the mix-up of standards which has led to greater enslavement of women. They have to look after the home, career and beauty. Definitions of beauty are constantly raised high. Chemical peeling of face, breast-implants and other plastic surgeries are in vogue. The burden is triple-fold. The male construction of female as an object of sex has been going on through a variety of forms of expression like, literature, sculpture, songs, paintings and photographs, dance forms, media etc. The fantasy world that veils experience of the female is the world of sex as seen through male eyes. The fantasies women take are male fantasies about women. Male eroticism is wedded to power.

Understanding of women's issues necessitates probing into the various dimensions of their social and cultural construction from a historical point of view. It further necessitates analysis of contextual variations. Any action for emancipation necessitates understanding of women's status. Thus, ethno-feminism becomes relevant in all formats and frames of movement and action for their empowerment. The need for radical restructuring is not denied but one cannot wait for total transformation nor use it as an argument against localized efforts for action related to specific areas for providing health care, education and employment to women and girls.

Social transformation is the end aim. However, there are specific issues, localized feministic sufferings, micro-level oppressions, prejudices in everyday life, set notions and fixed mindsets, which need to be taken up in the struggle for improvement, emancipation, conscientization and empowerment of women. This necessitates partnership of men, their involvement and their conscience building. Feminism need not lead to ideological isolation or alienation. The idea is not to beguile or sidetrack the issue. The effort is to create a new relationship between men and women based on equality, freedom, non-oppression and non-exploitation, so that the creative potentials of both are maximized as individuals and not as gender dichotomous categories.

The power of the producer over the reproducer and the concomitant 'ideological formulation' underlying this power must be seen as central to a theory of patriarchy. Such a theory of patriarchy, however fragmentary, lay dormant in Engels' treatise in *The Origin*. An obvious reason for this being the fact that Engels failed to subject the power structure located in the family to the same analysis he had so rigorously conducted in the case of power based on class. Ever since Engels' *The Origin*, new evidences from a wide array of studies done on the anthropology of family and kinship systems has provided adequate grounds to develop a theory of patriarchy that attempts to explain at the same time, both the subordination of women and class domination. Radical feminists first made use of the concept to understand sexual division of labour and society. According to them, there exists a patriarchal organization in society, determined essentially by a male hierarchical order that enjoys both economic and political power. It is the patriarchal organization, not class structure that defines women's position in the power hierarchy. Manifested through male force and control, the patriarchal system preserves itself through marriage and the family. Patriarchy then, is a sexual system of power, rooted in biology, i.e., in the women's reproductive role rather than in economics or history. There is, therefore, a departure from the use of class as an economic category to its use it as a sexual category.

Shulasmith Firestone presents the idea of sex class where women and men stand as two opposing classes. Capitalism was thus replaced with patriarchy as the oppressive system. The emancipation of women involved the destruction of the biological family as the basic form of social organization and the revolutionizing of reproductive technology that would free women from the biologically determined oppression. Kale Millett's theory of patriarchy, though not so biologistic, resembled that of Shulasmith's, in so far as it gave not only analytic independence to male domination but also analytic primacy. She argued that the political power that men wielded over women amounted to the fundamental political division in society. Our society, like all other civilizations, was based on patriarchy in which the rule of women by men was more rigorous than class stratification, more uniform, certainly more enduring.[4]

The theory of patriarchy then, as conceived by the radical feminists raises more problems than solving them. In trying to explain the domination of man over woman, it reduces woman's position in society to that of a biological reproductive unity. Patriarchy as a system of power and control is defined only in terms of sexual control of women by men. It is not possible to subsume a complex socially and historically constructed phenomenon under the simple category of biological difference. Secondly, if the subjugation of women is so naturally determined, then there is no possibility of change in such a given relationship. Lastly, such a reductionist position makes out men to be the natural enemies of women. Curiously, this turns radical feminism on its head, which then stands in danger of being nullified. Men are a part of the natural creation of the human race. The law of nature surely commands a mutual harmony at least at its most primitive level. It is not surprising that feminist philosophy is sometimes wrongly understood as being anti-male, thanks to the determinism of radical feminism.

Neither Marxism nor radical feminism can by itself explain convincingly the interrelationships between the material conditions of existing societies on the one hand and the ideological representations they hold on the other, with regard to women's oppression. A more scientific approach to the understanding of the problem may be sought in the synthesis of these two approaches, namely, socialist feminism. An endeavour towards such a synthesis has been attempted by Zillah Elisenstein. She perceives women's oppression in not only a historical materialistic explanation of society but also in the ideological underpinnings that society may perpetuate. If radical feminism conceived patriarchy in the framework of biology and Marxism in the framework of economics, then socialist feminism, as argued by Elisenstein, posits a sociology of patriarchy. Socialist feminism analyses power of men over women in terms of its class origins and patriarchal roots. In such an analysis, capitalism and patriarchy are neither autonomous nor identical systems; they are mutually dependent systems. Such a relationship between sex and class pitched in power or the converse, oppression, Elisenstein calls capitalist patriarchy.[5] But patriarchy as we know it today neither originated with capitalism nor will it end with it.

Elisenstein in her attempt to prove a scientific theory of patriarchy, distinguishes the concept of oppression from that of exploitation. She then proceeds to unfold the various ways by which sexual oppression is articulated within class exploitation under capitalism. Exploitation, according to her pertains to the economic reality of capitalist class relations for both men as well as women. In contradistinction to exploitation, oppression refers to women and minorities, defined within patriarchal, racist and capitalist relations. Under capitalism, men and women as workers in the labour force, are exploited whereas women's oppression arises not only from her exploitation as a wage labourer but also occurs from the sexual hierarchy obtained in society within as well as from without the family. Thus the concept of oppression embodies within it exploitation. Yet, it is not identical to exploitation as it represents a more complex social reality. In capitalist societies, a woman's oppression is not only derived from her role as a wage labourer but also as a mother, wife, domestic labourer and child-raiser.

If class is central to the Marxist theory of Capitalism, then power and oppression remain cardinal to a socialist feminist theory of patriarchy. Both Marx and Engels had seen man's oppression as a result of his exploitation as a worker in the capitalist society. According to them, women's oppression paralleled men's oppression. As members of the labour force, women experienced oppression as wage-salves and if and when relegated to the position of domestic labourer, they experienced oppression as a non-wage-slave. So women's oppression, unlike that of their male counterparts, is an instance of double oppression under capitalism. It is derived from production as well as reproduction. In Elisenstein's framework, patriarchy and capitalism are mutually dependent. As patriarchy provides the sexual hierarchical ordering of society for political control, 'capitalism as an economic class system derived by the pursuit of profit feeds off (this) patriarchal ordering.'[6] Capitalism preserves the family since family epitomizes the most basic sexual hierarchy and power therein.

Logically, therefore, in the strategy for transformation, socialist feminism locates political consciousness in the everyday oppression of women and their struggles. The importance of socialist feminist strategy derives from the daily struggle of women in production, reproduction and consumption. Elisentein criticizes male leftists and socialist women who naively believe that women as women cannot be organized because of their isolation in the home and their commitment to the cross-class mobilization around issues of abortion, healthcare, rape and child care. She suggests that where patriarchal controls subject women's lives to remarkably similar oppression across class differences, the strategy to reach all women for political action is at least worth a try.

Elisenstein's definition of patriarchy, theoretically informed that it precedes capitalism but rests in contemporary capitalism through the institutionalized hierarchy in the family. If patriarchy is an autonomous power system that cuts through different modes of production, what then is the material basis of such a system? Michele Barrett contends that 'the concept of patriarchy is one that does not resolve the problem of the analytic independence of "patriarchy" from capitalism.' The analysis vacillates between the assertion of patriarchy as a system of male power external to capitalism and the argument that the organization of patriarchal relations is functional for capitalism.[7] From Barrett's criticism, however, is evident the determinism that presupposes the existence of all ideology in a given society in the material basis of that society. If capitalism feeds on patriarchy, it does not necessitate the latter's origin in the material structure of capitalism *per se*. That patriarchy can well be external to capitalism and yet serve as an important means of oppression and exploitation under capitalism is reconcilable as shown in the work of the French anthropologist Calude Meillassoux.[8]

In his study of pre-capitalist social formations, Meillassoux explains the transformation from sex to gender in the reproductive mechanism of agricultural societies. Such a process transforms the biological differences between the sexes to social institutions based on relationships of super-ordination and subordination gender. Thus gender consequently entails power and control in society. Contrary to the radical feminist position that it rests on sexual differences between men and women, gender is a social and hierarchical ordering of institutions into strongly classified worlds of the male and the female. It is important to mention here that just as class remains the organizational basis of capitalism, similarly gender constitutes the hierarchical principle of patriarchy. Thus the material basis of patriarchy has to be sought in the emergence of gender. The subordination of women cannot entirely be explained within the problematic of the origins of private property. To the extent that gender may be said to precede class societies and the institution of private property, there may, however, be a historical relationship between gender and class.

The origins of patriarchy in social reproduction may be undermined by the modern industrial production. As a matter of fact, Kathleen Gough, a great sociologist, rightly points out that the modes of social reproduction cease to be a basis for female subordination when artificial birth control, spaced births, small families, patent feeding and communal nurseries allow it to be shared by both the sexes. Modern technology and cybernation removes most of the heavy work for which women are not physically as well equipped as men. While modern capitalism has perpetuated patriarchy, it perhaps also has by its own technological and scientific developments created the basis for the end of patriarchy.

But technological and material development by itself cannot overcome the age old power based gender relations in society. Equality between the sexes necessitates a radical transformation of the power structure in society. Strategies for social transformation on class lines cannot bring about the desired changes in the gender relations. There is a need therefore to reckon with gender and underlying patriarchy of male dominance in contemporary capitalism. This requires us to take excursions into theory and history.

Coming to the case of women in India and the theoretical foundations of patriarchy here, normative Brahmanical view on women is that she is subordinate to man and accepts her pre-conceived, pre-determined role as a faithful wife and selfless mother. As Neera and Maithreyi puts in right words:

> The Indian society like a number of 'classical' societies was patriarchal. Patriarchal values regulating sexuality, reproduction and social production (meaning total conditions of production) prevailed and were expressed through specific cultural metaphors and other rules prohibiting women from specific activities and denying certain rights did exist. But subtler expression of patriarchy was through symbolism giving messages of inferiority of women through legends highlighting the self-sacrificing, self-effacing pure image of women and through ritual practices which day in and day out emphasized the dominant role of a woman as faithful wife and devout mother.[9]

The wife was always viewed in these sacred texts as an assistant to her husband in fulfilling religious vows and performing *dharma*.

In Vedas and Epics, we come across the names of learned ladies like Gargi, Maitreyi, Kausalya, Tara, Sulabha, Draupadi and so on. But women were not accorded equal status at every level of social interaction. Women in fact were treated as a thing or property but never treated as self-dependent beings in any civilization. Draupadi's case is an example of it. Women's independence was discouraged in almost all the civilizations and religions. Without women, in fact, there would have been no civilization, no religion and no men.

Kapadia's study about the status of women in ancient India clearly reveals the gender-disparity existing at that time and the nature of the perspective of ancient law givers towards sex inequality. The Bhagavad Gita, considers the woman as a Shudra. Again, in the Sankara-rites performed as marriage ritual, it is offspring, particularly the birth of a male child, that is the recurring theme."[10]

Manu enunciates the ideal of wifehood as in essence

meaning the negation of her personality. The husband must constantly be worshipped as a God by the faithful wife (*Sadhvi*), even if he be destitute of character or seeking pleasure elsewhere or devoid of good qualities. A good wife desirous of living in this as well as in the next world with her husband, must never do anything that would displease him, either alive or dead. A woman attains paradise "not by virtue of any austere penance but as a result of her obedience and devotion to her husband. Women have no sacrifices or fasts ordained for them. Neither are they allowed to perform the *Sraddha*. To serve and worship their husband with respect and obedience is their only duty. By the fulfillment of that duty alone they succeed in attaining heaven."[11] Manu says that even in the home nothing should be done by a child, a young or even an old wife (women) independently. Kapadia writes:

> In order to justify the low status which he is out to assign to woman, Manu confirms and stresses the prejudicial view in respect of her sexual appetite. Women must particularly be guarded against evil inclinations, they will bring sorrow on both the families. Considering it the highest duty of all castes, even weak husbands must strive to guard their wives."[12]

It is notable that Manu accuses woman, just because she is a woman. "If she be chaste it is because she has not found a proper man, place or opportunity."[13] It is the nature of women to seduce man in this world. She is able to lead astray not only the ignorant but even a learned man and make him a slave of lust. It is hence that she is called a *pramade*, a temptress. "Woman was created for infatuating man and hence there is nothing more heinous than women."[14] Love of scandal and the lust for sex the creator gave to women. A man can never guard them by words, blows or punishments of various kinds for they are unbridled. "A man with hundred tongues, even if he were to do nothing else but lecture upon the vilest defects of woman, would not finish them in a long life of a hundred years."[15] Through their passion for men, their unstable temper and inherent heartlessness, they become disloyal to their husbands, however, carefully they may be guarded in this world. Manu therefore, wants women to be under the surveillance of her father in her childhood, her husband in her youth and her son on the death of her husband. "A woman would never think of independence from the father, the husband or the sons because by so doing she will make both the families contemptible."[16]

During the *Bhakti* cult (during 13-16th centuries), the idea of equality between man and woman and man to man was emphasized. Every human being was considered sparks of the one supreme deity.[17] But still even during these periods woman was considered a great obstruction in the way of spiritual realization.

In colonial period, there were several reformers who started questioning the subordinate position of women in India. Raja Rammohan Roy fixed his attention on *Sati* and enforced widowhood. Like Raja Rammohan Roy, several other social reformers like Ishwarchand Vidyasagar, M. G. Rnanade, Mahatma Phule, Lokhitwad, Maharshi Karve and so on came forward to annihilate injustice done towards women. They tackled the issues of *Sati*, fate of widow, widow remarriage, polygamy, child-marriage, denial of property rights and education to women. They thought that removal of these disabilities will pave the way for equality between the sexes. But by and large, women's condition remained the same, as Vijay Agnew points out that participation in politics did not change the ideal of Hindu womanhood. The role of a wife and mother continued to be idealized and women continued to accept and abide by the conventional image.[18] She further points out that social reform movement of the 19th century and nationalist movement of the first half of 20th century helped the elite group of women to enjoy freedom. "But for society as a whole, sex roles, stereotype images and the Indian woman's conception of herself or her role in life remained virtually unchanged."[19]

The Indian women's movement can be classified as a bourgeois feminist movement, along with the women's rights movement of United States and Great Britain. Bourgeois feminist movements are composed of middle class women who campaign for the extension of educational opportunities, voting rights and property rights to women. These are the privileges enjoyed by middle class men and are important for the exercise of power by middle class women in society.[20]

After independence the constitution and the legal measures that followed tried to bring about equality of the sexes as it was thought that law could change the society. The constitution guarantees social, economic and political justice to all. Article 15(6) tilts towards justice to women. The enactment of Hindu Marriage and Inheritance Act, the Termination of Pregnancy Act, the Minimum Wages Act etc., clearly reveal that the state wants equality of the sexes in several spheres. But the status report on women which was brought out in 1975 states adverse sex-ratio, growing dominance of violence in the domestic sphere, dowry deaths, rape cases, *sati* etc., and explodes the myth of sexuality in India.

> Neera and Maithreyi point out that Patriarchal values and normative structures established some two thousand years ago still persist though in different garb. Motherhood and the ideal of a faithful, loyal self-sacrificing wife are projected through the media and the education system. The reality of subordinate position of woman is indicated through adverse sex-ratio of girls, the growing domestic violence, increasing number of dowry deaths and rape cases.[21]

An overview of the entire span of more than 2000 years reveals that women are on the receiving end in India. They were never thought of as independent individuals taking their own decision, and gender disparity is socially enforced. Never the state or any other organization raised the fundamental question basic to gender inequality. Whenever some problems such as unequal sex-ratio etc., came on the surface, certain laws were made or modified to mitigate the evil. But the basic issues were never questioned. Social scientists too have rarely come forward to analyze the situation in its proper perspective.

When I critically reflect upon the different theories of feminism, I cannot but find fundamental disagreements among the theorists. Some feminists believe that all women are as physically capable as men. Some feminists do not believe in this view. They rather support the view that there are biological differences between men and women but highlight women's special qualities like kindness, caring and affirm that they have more fine qualities than men. Some feminists focus on individual autonomy, rights, liberty, independence and diversity but do not focus on how conflicting cases of men and women pertaining to their autonomy, rights, liberty should be resolved. Some feminists say that women can be liberated only by improving their material or economic conditions and not their cultural conditions. Some feminists think that feminism is no longer viable. Some feminists advocate that in order to be equal with men, women must be granted some special privileges and men should not be an issue in feminism. Some others view oppression of women as the most fundamental form of oppression, one that cuts across boundaries of race, culture and economic groups. They draw lines between biologically determined behaviour and culturally determined behaviour in order to free women. Some other feminists advocate separatism from men and others degrade men in all matters and glorify women. While feminists disagree about the nature of and solutions to the subordination of women, all feminists agree that women's oppression, exploitation and subordination exists in the society which is morally wrong and must be abolished.

Feminists have thus always sought to improve the quality of women's lives by diminishing the exploitations, abuses and oppressions that afflict women. Ending work place discrimination against women, increasing women's participation in government and economy, securing women's reproductive freedom, reducing violence against women, fostering a female-centred eroticism, achieving equal rights, eliminating cultural misogamy and ending the sexual exploitation of women are suggested as some of the basic goals of feminists everywhere, which they have been trying to achieve. The attacks on feminists are misguided. Feminists do not hate the family, men and sex. They hate only exploitation, oppression, subordination and discrimination done against them on various unjustified grounds. They want that women should be given autonomy to shape their own life as they like. They should not be treated as property, but as individuals.

REFERENCES

1. Supriya Akerkar, "Theory and Practice of Women's Movement in India," *Economic and Political Weekly*, Vol.XXX, No.17, pp.2-3
2. *Ibid.*, pp.2-4
3. Ruchi Banthiya, *From Historicity to Postmodernity* (Jaipur: Rawal, 1994) pp.139-143
4. Schulasmith Firestone, *The Dialectic of Sex* (New York: Bantam Books, 1970) p.38
5. *Ibid.*, p.22
6. *Ibid.*, p.28
7. Michele Barrett, *Women's Oppression Today* (London: Verso, 1980) p.13
8. Cloude Meillassoux, *Maidens, Meal and Money* (Cambridge: Cambridge University Press, 1981)
9. Neera Desai and Maithreyi Krishmaraj, *Women and Society in India* (Delhi: Ajanta Publications, 1987)

10. K. M. Kapadia, *Marriage and Family in India* (Bombay: Oxford University Press, 1958) p.252
11. *Ibid.*, p.253
12. *Ibid.*, p.254
13. *Ibid.*
14. *Ibid.*
15. *Ibid.*, p.255
16. *Ibid.*
17. *Ibid.*
18. Vijay Agnew, *Elite Women in Indian Politics* (New Delhi: Vikas Publishing House, 1979) p.61
19. *Ibid.*
20. J. M. Everett, *Women and Social Change in India* (New Delhi: Heritage Publishers, 1978) p.191
21. *Ibid.*, p.8

3

Status of Women

One way to judge the rights enjoyed by Indian women or the rights they are deprived off is to study their status. In reality the status of women represents the rights women of any age are deprived off or the rights they enjoy. However, to draw a conclusion about the position of women is a difficult and complicated problem. It is, therefore, necessary to trace this position in the historical perspective.

In the course of Indian history from prehistoric to modern and contemporary times there were distinct stages of the rise and fall in the status and role of women in India. The recorded evidence found in a certain period and in a particular place/province has expressed opposite views about the worth, nature and importance of women. According to one school, a woman is the best gift of God to man. She brings prosperity when she is properly treated and respected, and is called Lakshmi, the goddess of wealth and prosperity. The second school of thought holds the view that the best way to reach God is to avoid women.[1] Sage Agastya says: "Women combine the fickleness of the lightning, the sharpness of a weapon and the swiftness of the eagle."[2] Altekar says that to ascertain the position of women in Hindu society, one should study the position of women in peace and war times. During wars, the attitude of society towards women was very unsympathetic particularly if the women had the misfortune of falling into the hands of the enemies. They found it impossible to get readmitted into their family and society. A study of ancient literature reveals that even during peace times the position of women was not very satisfactory. The status of women was considered to be equal to that of the Sudras and killing of women was not considered as a disgraceful act. The literature of Indian history abounds with contradictory and conflicting views on the status of women. It can properly be understood within the socio-cultural condition of the society. As Majumdar has rightly said, "The status of women in India can be more understood in the Indian ethnology than in that of religion or Brahmanism..."[3] The contradictory views about women's status are because of the emergence of the ideals of womanhood at different times. It appears that originally Hindu society had a flexible social structure. The concept of '*ardhangini*' suggests that there was equality between men and women; neither of the two being superior to the other.[4] Later on, barbarous practices developed and women were relegated to a subordinate status.[5]

The status enjoyed by the Indian woman cannot easily be assessed. While the 'ideal' was worshipped, the 'real' was neglected. Cormack asserts: "Traditional India has always accorded woman a high place and indeed equality."[6] Gorwaney also observes that "Ideally, women were accepted as a living force in society, the embodiment of '*Shakti*' and a symbol of purity, religiousness, spirituality and sacrifice."[7] In practice, however, they were subjected to suppression and many deprivations were thrust on them by men. They were denied equal rights in marital, familial, social, educational, economic and political fields. They were assigned with a subordinate status.

According to Mehta, there is recorded evidence to show that woman was not always without rights nor was she constantly in subjection. There is, however, greater evidence to show that the contrary was even more true; for many centuries her position continued to be one in which she did not have either legal or social rights to make her independent of the family into which she was born or married.[8] She further remarks that the status of woman is a complex question and has to be studied as an integral part of the socio-economic structure in which women live. It cannot be dissociated from it. The changes that have taken place in their position are a part of the process of transformation of a traditional society.

Altekar argues that the position which women occupied in Hindu society at the dawn of civilization during the Vedic Age is much better than what we ordinarily expect it to have been. He further says that even before the Aryans came to India in about 2000 B.C., there is evidence to believe that Indian women shared a responsible position with men and played an important role in evolving a definite culture and tradition. Their status excelled that of the contemporary civilizations of ancient Greece, Rome and even early Christianity.[9] There is almost a consensus of opinion among great scholars of classical literature that during the age of the Vedas (2500-1500 B.C) a woman's status was equivalent to that of man. The position of women in Vedic period can be judged by the way in which the birth of a girl was received. None of the hymns of *Rigveda* considered the birth of a daughter as inauspicious. But we find prayers for the birth of a son in *Atharva Veda* which says, "The birth of a girl, grant it elsewhere; here grant a boy."[10] We do find a frequent longing for a male child in the *Rigveda*, while during the Vedic Age, there were some parents who would perform *Kanyâsrâddhas* on the second day of the moon for the blessing of getting learned and capable daughters. The *Rigveda* praises the father of many daughters. Besides, it was recommended that "*Matrika-Puja*" should take place first; the '*Kumari Puja*' was performed at the end of all Vedic rituals.[11]

Initiation of girls was common. Girls were educated like boys. Like their brothers the girls wore the sacred thread (*Upavita-Dharana*) and used to pass through a period of *Brahmacharya*. After this *Upavita* ceremony, the Vedic women carried on the study of the Vedas, recited Vedic mantras, performed Vedic rites and rituals, undertook vows and did whatever was necessary for the proper performance of *yagayajna*, just like a son. According to *Sarvanukra-manika* there were as many as twenty women who are credited with having composed the hymns of the *Rigveda*. Many of them became distinguished poetesses and where honoured by having their poems included in Vedic literature. Some of the high class women were highly educated and they actively participated in intellectual and philosophical discussions. Apart from a literary career, women entered fields of teaching, medicine, business, defence and administration.[12]

The marriage of girls used to take place at the age of understanding, i.e., between 14-17 years and that too with their consent. The educated girls had naturally an effective voice in the selection of their life partners. Pre-puberty marriages were unknown as there were *Swayamvara* marriages, where women were given the chance of selecting their partners. There were also many instances of love marriages. It can be concluded that both men and women had considerable freedom in selecting their partners though parents often arranged a suitable match.[13] If for any reason a daughter remained unmarried, she was expected to live under the protection of her father, and after her father's death under the control and protection of her brother. Otherwise, she was on her own. Perpetual tutelage of women is of a later origin.[14]

The position of a daughter during the Vedic period did not suffer much from authoritative interference. She was socialized with a high degree of modesty.[15] She was expected to have tolerance, patience, submission to and an identification of her personality with her husband's. She, in turn, received affection, consideration and regard. Though marriage was of great social and religious significance it was not mandatory as there were some reference to girls who remained unmarried.[16]

Ordinarily, a daughter did not have any right to hold, acquire or dispose of property. This means that she did not enjoy any legal status in the *Rigvedic* times. But the unmarried daughter who stayed on in her father's house got a share of his property. She could not claim a share in her brother's property as it is clearly laid down in the *Rigveda* that "a son born of the body does not transfer wealth to sister."[17] Married daughter could inherit their father's property only in the absence of a brother.[18] The social or familial status of the daughter was fairly Satisfactory in the *Rigvedic* period.

The Vedic society also was patriarchal and male-dominated. The household was ruled by a house lord, who wielded almost absolute control over all other members of the family and to him his wife or wives were bound by a strict tie of lifelong duty and obedience.[19] Marriage, in fact, was a religious necessity for both men and women; but neither could reach heaven without being accompanied by his or her duly married spouse. The Vedic women being *Sahadharmini* or *Patni* had the fullest right to participate in all the religious ceremonies with her husband. She could also perform sacrifice independently and was not regarded as an impediment in religious pursuits. Her position was an honoured one in the family. She was the joint-owner of the household with her husband though in actual practice she was the subordinate partner. This was because of the prevalence of a patriarchal family system as it is today. Her social status is not only that of a loving wife but also of a loving mother. She was described by the Vedic sages as an ornament of the home. She enjoyed absolute equality with men in matters of religion.[20]

The *Dharmashastra* has raised a chaste wife to the rank of a goddess. Out of love and veneration, she has been placed above the father and teacher. The *Panchatantra* mentions that the maintenance of a home is known by the culture of the wife; without her, a home is like a forest. *Rigveda* accords a high position to women. As mothers, the Vedic women held a far more venerable position than a man as the father.

During this period asceticism was not of great prominence. Women had the right of free movement. Polygamy prevailed to some extent among the rich and royal families but ordinarily monogamy was the rule. The main disadvantage from which the wife suffered in the Vedic age was that she could neither hold nor inherit property. It appears that under certain Aryan customs the property rights in some kind of properties which women slowly acquired were assimilated with their rights in their portion of the bride-price, probably as being the only existing type of woman's property.[21] The recognition of woman's property with absolute rights (*stridhana*) was of a later origin.

In the post Vedic period, women were known to take up teaching career. She was accepted as an *Acharya*. Some of the lady teachers were specialists in theology and philosophy, the most abstruse and difficult subjects. Women had the privilege of adoption. For instance, Vadharimati adopted Haranyashasta and Loppada adopted Santha, the daughter of Dasaratha.[22]

The position of women during the Vedic age is clearly manifest from the *Suklas* of revered *Nari Risis* or women seers in the *Rigveda*. Women as daughters, sisters, wives and mothers had an equally honoured place in the family, society and state alike. Thus, in all aspects they had equal rights with men and were their equal partners, friends and helpers all through.

Though the Hindus of the Vedic period had a patriarchal

society, the women in general did not suffer from disabilities which are characteristic of later periods. This is particularly true of widows. Widows of this age were permitted to remarry. This practice seems to have been accepted as normal from the Vedic period onwards. A number of references are found in the Vedas to show that widow remarriage was common, though the remarried widow could not aspire for the status of '*Grihini*' (wife), whereby she could become the mistress of the house. The use of the word '*parapurva*', a woman who has had a second husband proves that widows were remarried. The word '*Didhishu*' used in the *Rigveda* means the second husband of a woman. *Atharva* Veda refers to a '*Punarbha*', showing that marriage of a widow was not opposed. The custom of a widow marrying the brother of her deceased husband seems to have been common. Hence, the word '*Devara*' which means a woman's brother-in-law, literally the second husband.

The institution of *Niyoga* (Levirate) came into Aryan society from some non-Aryan source. Under the system of *Niyoga*, a widow or a woman whose husband was not virile was allowed to have conjugal relations with her brother-in-law, who was regarded as the most eligible person for this duty, or some other near relation till she gave birth to an offspring. A widow was allowed to have two sons through *Niyoga*. A son by levirate was always preferred to a son by adoption.[23]

We do not find any reference to *Sati* or burning of widows in *Rigveda*. On the other hand, Vedic hymns refer to remarriage of widows rather than their self-immolation. The burning of the widow on the funeral pyre of her husband might have been practised by the early Aryans. But in reality in the Rigvedic period the widow was made to lie by the side of her dead husband. She was, however, asked to come down and a prayer was offered that she be granted a prosperous life enjoying the bliss of children and wealth.[24]

Attachment of importance to the birth of a male child became responsible for the gradual decline in the status of women. The widow was given an inferior position as she was unfortunate enough to lose the all powerful protecting male partner.

The custom of widow remarriage as we understand the term today did not exist. But even then we have some references to widow remarriage with the younger brother or with the next kinsman of her deceased husband. It can only be said that her life was not bound by so many restrictions and austerities as it was in the later times. She had not to ascend her husband's funeral pyre.[25] In other words, *Sati* system was not in practice. The right of Niyoga shows how a widow was very liberally treated in those days. The legal status of the widow was the same as that of the wife. The widow, however, did not have the right to hold property. But then, even a married wife did not possess that right.

From about 1500 B.C., there were perceptible changes in the women's status due to various reasons, among which the most important was the denial of education. Traces of deterioration are found in all periods following 1500 B.C but it became much more marked after the beginning of the Christian era and reached its peak after the Mongol invasion in the tenth century.

With the lapse of time the position of the daughter also changed. During this period there was a gradual decline in women's education. Girls were not allowed to go to the houses of the preceptor or centres of education but were taught only by near relatives like father, brother or the uncle. Thereafter only the girls of rich and cultured families received religious and other training. As a result, there appeared a tendency to curtail the religious rights and privileges of women in general. During this period, the desire to get a son to provide for the future became quite intense and daughters came to be looked upon as encumbrances. Girls were married off at around the age of 16 and they had some voice in the selection of their life partners. Love marriages were also common. Among the *Kshatriyas*, *swayamvara* was fairly a common practice. The social and familial status of the daughter deteriorated in the post-Vedic period. Her proprietary right was also the same as it was in the Vedic age. Even so far as her right in the separate property of the father was concerned, she was not altogether ignored.[26] The following line aptly depicts the position of the daughter: "A wife is a comrade, a daughter is a misery and a son a light in the highest heaven."[27]

According to *Gautam Samhita* a girl should be given in marriage before she attains puberty. He who neglects it, commits sin. Some declare that a girl should be given in marriage before she wears clothes.[28] *Vasistha Samhita* also says the same thing.[29]

There was a slight improvement with respect to women's right to property as these *slokas* make it clear. For example, Manu says: "As if self, son and a daughter is equal to a son, how then when one's self is living in the form of one's daughter, can anyone else take the wealth.'[30] Brahaspati says: "The wife is declared to be the inheritor of the husband's wealth and in default of her, the daughter; the daughter, like a son springs from the limb of a man; how can any other man inherit her father's property while she lives?"[31]

The daughters could only succeed that property if she were a widow or in default of the son, grandson, great grandson. But in normal circumstances, she could get one-fourth share of the property. Manu says: 'but to the maiden (sister) the brothers shall severally give (portions) out of their share, one-fourth parts, those who refuse to give (it) will become outcastes.'[32] Yajnavalkya also says: 'but sisters should be disposed of in marriage giving them as an allotment the fourth share.'[33]

The intention of the *Smriti* writers was not to make woman

a shareholder in the son's property but just to reserve some wealth necessary for her marriage. But the daughter's right of succession in her father's property cannot be said to be satisfactory.

There were gradual changes in the position of women in this period. Women were not allowed to participate in the performance of sacrificial ceremonies. They eventually began to lose touch with the Vedas and were pushed back to domestic duties. The study of Vedas became the monopoly of men. Women also ceased to attend public meetings. Having lost their importance as comrades of men in public activities, they came to be honoured merely as mothers.

The reason for the deteriorating of women's status was the intermarriages between the Aryans and the Dravidians. The non-Aryan wife, with her ignorance of the Sanskrit language and Hindu religion, obviously could not enjoy the same religious privileges as the Aryan consort.[34] The black non-Aryan wife could be her husband's associate in pleasure but not in religious rituals, says several authorities.

The discontinuance of *Upanayana*, the neglect of education and lowering of the marriage age produced disastrous consequences regarding the position and status of women. Early marriage became a hindrance in the education of girls. Women came to be regarded as being of the same status as the *Sudra*. During this period, on the one hand women were being idealized, and on the other she was given a very degraded status.[35]

Over the property of her husband it was generally considered that a woman had no right during his lifetime beyond the right of maintenance and residence. According to the *Mitakshara* law, in the matter of partition, a wife was allowed to get an equal share with her own son or sons when the division took place in the lifetime of her husband. But she could not herself demand a partition. She could get a share only if the husband himself separated from his sons during his lifetime or if the sons claimed partition during the father's lifetime.[36] Though a woman had her own property called *Stridhana*, she was given only limited ownership. It seems that the spirit of the Hindu law was not to allow women independence to dispose of property, but merely the right to possess and enjoy property.[37] It can be said that the social status of the wife was not satisfactory. However, her status improved in the sphere of proprietary right.

The deterioration in the status of widows commenced from the epic period. Widowhood was considered both undesirable as well as inauspicious. The position of widows became more pitiable because the *sutras* ordered a widow to avoid, for the duration of a year, the use of honey, meat, spirits and liquor as well as salt and sleep on the ground. At the expiry of six months, she could, with the permission of her Guru, bear a son by her brother-in-law in case she had no son. The custom of *Niyoga* came into existence during this period. Remarriages are not found among the Aryan widows but there are instances of non-Aryan widows marrying Aryans. The *Mahabharata* says that a child widow can remarry, and her sons by the second marriage can offer oblations to the gods.[38] The children by the second marriage of a widow were given a social as well as religious status. Child widows, therefore, married without fear of social ostracism. However, during this period, *Niyoga* was preferred to widow re-marriage.

The custom of widow burning came into existence around 400 AD. Though there were instances of widows surviving their husbands and offering them funeral oblations, on the whole the position of widows was not so honourable during this period. The rise of Brahamanism during the *Smriti* period became detrimental to the status of women. The Hindu law-givers of this period imposed certain duties on the widows, who did not ascend the funeral pyre and chose instead to survive the husband. All the sages, prescribe a life of strict discipline and penance on such widows for their whole life.

The custom of *Niyoga* was condemned by the Smriti writers when chastity became the main qualification for marriage. Manu disapproved of the custom of '*Niyoga*' and declared that it was fit for cattle only. Although it is still practised in some communities in India, the custom appears very strange and unacceptable to the modern mind.[39]

Widow marriage was prohibited. The practice of '*Sati*' was recommended by many of the authorities and was well established by the end of 6th century A.D. The practice prevailed as early as Alexander's invasion about 325 B.C. Travelers like Strabo, Megasthenes and Diodarus who accompanied Alexander, allude to this practice. The law-givers forced the widows to lead a life of austerities, fasting and abstinence from pleasure. Manu, the Hindu law-giver, says: (i) Until her death, let her be patient of hardships, self-controlled, and chaste and strive to fulfill that most excellent duty which is prescribed for wives who have one husband only. (ii) Let her emancipate her body by living on pure flowers, roots and fruits but she must never mention the name of another man after the husband has died. (iii) A virtuous wife, who after the death of her husband, constantly remains chaste, reaches heaven though she has no son, just like those chaste men.[40]

The codes of the Hindu law commanded that a widow should lead a chaste life. Loss of chastity of the widow affected not only her social status but also her proprietary position. But the injunctions to emancipate her body and to live on a frugal diet were in the nature of a religious or moral injunction.

Unjust and archaic social customs like child marriage, *Sati* and polygamy reduced the status of women to the level of mere goods or cattle. They were regarded as '*nari-sudras*'. The status of widows was still more inferior. Altekar says that the period between 500 A.D to 1800 A.D was one of progressive deterioration in the position of women. In the history of India, these depressing days of total injustice, intolerance and inequality would remain as the darkest spots for ever. There were varied and many reasons for the deterioration in the position of women. The only good thing that developed during this period was the recognition of certain proprietary rights for women.[41]

Chaudhury has stated that women of India rose to the heights of knowledge and realization, worked with men in all spheres of life and even surpassed them in many respects and were entitled to the fullest freedom as well as to untrammeled self-dependence and self-determination. Such bold and blessed self-confident and independent women found themselves suddenly confined within four walls of dark and dreary homes, with their minds desolate and depressing with almost all their fundamental birthrights totally or almost cut off. They were deprived of any rights to justice, freedom, education, equality and were degraded domestically, socially, legally, economically, politically and in every other way. They came to be called *Abala* (the powerless) or *Griha-pinjarakokil* (cuckoo of the home cage) and subject to the most derogatory maxim: '*Putrartha kriyate bharya*' (women has to be taken in marriage for procreation only.)[42]

There are contradictory views regarding the position and status of women. While some of the earlier authorities have described women as abodes of more evil than good, the progressive and liberal thinkers were in favour of women. They have gone to the extent of worshipping her as a living image of the Divine Mother. In *Manu Smriti* we find two contradictory statements: (i) Where women are honoured, there gods dwell. (ii) A woman is to be protected and sheltered all through her life by her male relatives – by the father during her childhood, the husband when a housewife and the son during her widowhood. The position of women in all other spheres, except the proprietary rights, continued to deteriorate in this period. Most of the causes responsible for the degradation of women during the last period continued to operate in this age also. The age of marriage was fixed at eight. The *Upanayana* ceremony of girls was completely discontinued. The commentators were of the opinion that the parents would be committing sin, if the girl's age exceeded eight years. Only in *Kshatriya* families girls were married off at the age of 14 or 15. Girls of rich families, however, still received education and few of them distinguished themselves as poetesses and critics. The ignorance of most girls created a tendency among men to treat them lightly and pass cynical remarks about their weakness and worthlessness.[43] Unjust and stupid social customs like child marriage, *Sati* and polygamy reduced the status of women to the level of mere goods or cattle. They were regarded as *Nari-Sudras*.

Gradually, the practice of marrying off child-widows was stopped. Permission to the child-widows to remarry was withdrawn during this period. In the beginning of 1000 A.D only widows from the higher strata of society were not allowed to marry, but in course of time the custom got extended to the lower sections also in the hope of attaining respectability. Widows were ordained to lead a strict ascetic life. An ascetic generally removes the hair on the head. The custom of disfiguring the Hindu widow appears to have originated from this. During 11th century the cruel custom of *Sati* was widely practised. Most of the widows voluntarily ascended the funeral pyres of their husbands because of the cruel and tiresome life they would be required to lead as widows. Sometimes, the cruel relatives of the widows burned them forcibly, because they were either afraid that the widows might misbehave and bring disgrace to the family or wanted to misappropriate her share in the family property.[44] Consequently, the practice of *Sati* or *jauhar* became quite common and popular particularly in North India.[45]

By 1200 A.D the widow's right to inherit the share of her husband's property came to be recognized all over the country.

The recognition of the right of inheritance was thus a blessing to the poor widows. The daughter comes as the next heir to the widow. Manu placed the daughter in the fifth position.

In the Muslim period, that is, in the 11th century onwards, the position of women further deteriorated. Women faced a number of hardships and cruelty due to evil practices like child marriage, the *purdah* system, *sati*, widowhood, prostitution and the *deva dasi* system. As Hate mentions, "The advent of the Muslims arrested the progress of Hindu civilization and an era of blind faith and perpetuation of old customs followed."[46]

Hindu women, like their Muslim counterparts, adopted the *purdah*. In Northern India this practice was very rigorously enforced. As Sridevi says:

> Most women, being subject to *purdah*, had no opportunity for education. They remained somewhere in between the two portals, with no education, no special privileges but simplicity, patience, perseverance, endurance, understanding, immense love for home and children and intense religious inclinations adorned them.[47]

During this period, the role of women conformed to the dictum laid down by Manu, the great law giver of second century that 'a woman does not deserve freedom' and that her life should throughout be one of dependence on man. Another similar dictum laid down by him was that a woman should be subservient in all stages of her life: in childhood to the father, in youth to the husband and his elderly kin and to the sons when widowed.[48] Among the traditional Hindu families the fate of woman, especially of the daughters-in-law, was always of subordination to all other members.[49] The position of the daughter in Hindu society reached its nadir as child marriage was a popular practice of the social life of the Mughal period. Hindu daughters too were married before the age of nine or ten and in some cases were married even before they had learnt to talk.[50] The legal position of Hindu women with regard to inheritance was again unsatisfactory. Women were excluded from succession to property and made dependent on men.[51] Due to early marriage, girls were deprived of education. All these social circumstances led to the further deterioration in the position of daughters.

Along with the insecurity and uncertainty which prevailed in the Mughal period, the practice of *purdah* became rigid and women were forbidden even to visit the holy shrines. Both Hindu and Muslim women lost all their liberal activities and became the property of their male masters. The practice of *purdah*, invented to protect women, had a restrictive effect. As a result, the social life of women narrowed down.[52]

Widow re-marriage was prohibited in general. Altekar says that the prohibition of widow remarriage began to be imposed from about 1000 A.D., even on the child widows. It was totally prohibited in Hindu society from about 1100 A.D. Initially, upper caste widows were prohibited from remarrying whereas lower caste widows were allowed to do so.[53] Since the 1st century, the lower castes, due to sanskritisation and the desire to increase their respectability, began to impose upon themselves the prohibition of widow remarriage.

The practice of tonsuring of widows was prevalent among many high castes until recently. It is believed to have come into vogue in about the 8th century A.D. This system of tonsuring was adopted by the Brahmins under the influence of Buddhism as the Buddhist nuns underwent tonsure in imitation of the monks.[54] However, Kare suggests that a widow was tonsured just as the sons of a deceased man underwent tonsure as a matter of purification and as a symbol of bereavement.[55] From 12th century A.D onwards, the tonsure of widows became prevalent all over India. It was common more in the South than in the North of the country. Though the cruel practice is dying out, it is still prevalent among some orthodox sects of Brahmins in Southern India.

Once widow marriage was prohibited, society desired to make the widow as unattractive as possible so that no man could even want to marry her. With this idea in mind, the widow was tonsured and made to wear white clothes only. The idea might probably have been borrowed from the Buddhist or Jain nuns who wore white clothes, when they renounced the worldly life, since the widow too was supposed to have renounced the world. She was forbidden to wear any jewel. She had to sleep on the bare floor and partake of a frugal meal cooked by herself only once a day. This deprived her of good health and good looks, so that even if she wanted to remarry no man came forward to do so. Even Vedvyasa opines that 'if a widow does not become a *sati*, she should shave her head.'[56] Widows had to follow strict rules and restrictions. So, they frequently preferred *Sati* to the tiresome life prescribed for them. Most widows voluntarily ascended the funeral pyres of their husbands.

Henry Maine opines that superstitious beliefs, coupled with the Brahmanical dislike for the enjoyment of property by women, had led to the practice of *sati* and was intended to fight the ancient rule of civil law, which made woman a tenant for life in respect of her husband's property.[57] It is also believed that the custom came into practice due to frequent wars and foreign invasions which left behind widows who preferred to commit *sati* to leading a life of disgrace or dishonour. However, though it started as a voluntary gesture, as time went by, many cases were reported where widows were forcibly cast into the flames of the pyre much against their will.[58]

Sati became more frequent among the royal families in Northern India, and quite common in Kashmir during the period 1500 to 1800 A.D. The practice of *sati* or *jauhar* was also quite common as well as popular particularly among the

Rajputs and Marathas of Central India.[59] The incentives before a *sati* were the beliefs like she who follows her husband in death, will dwell in heaven for 3.5 crore years, as Sankha and Angirasa say.[60] Several Muslim emperors discouraged *sati* and adopted measures to prevent it as far as possible, but did not succeed. This era led not only to the degeneration of women's physical, mental and social life, but her rights in educational, social, religious and economic fields were also lowered gradually.

The legal position of Hindu women with regard to inheritance rights was also unsatisfactory. Under the doctrine of *Stridhana* they were generally excluded from succession to property and this led to their dependence on men.[61] Denial of education produced far-reaching effects on the status and role of women. The subordinate position of women became an accepted cultural norm for the majority of society until the beginning of the nineteenth century.

From time to time, reform movements like Buddhism, Jainism, Vaishnavism, Veerashaivism and Sikhism made sincere efforts to improve the status of women. They too regarded women as mothers and wives but necessarily inferior to men. Buddhism considered male monks superior to the nuns. In Jainism, though women were given a respectable position in congregational life, they were condemned severely. In the 12th century, Veerashaivism permitted their women the right to divorce and remarry. The *Bhakti* movement also played an important role in raising the status of women by allowing them to seek spiritual solace independently. The little but powerful orthodox force in the society erased the good effects brought about by these revolutions. In the history of India, 18th century was a period of all round decline. It was the darkest period so far as women were concerned. Political decay following the disruption of the Mughal empire and disorder due to the advent of various European powers, combined with fossilized customs, traditions, superstitions and irrational bigotry ruined the nation. Under the new conditions, women lost their independent identity. They did not enjoy a separate world of their own. Until quite recently their very existence was merely a bare necessity and taken to be an indispensable appendage to the male population. They were totally and forcefully subjugated to male superiority, physically and intellectually.[62]

In the latter half of the 18th century, when the British came to India, women's status had dropped to the lowest level. It was the worst period in the history of the country because of child marriage and *sati* system. A. L. De'Souza says:

> Women were denied equal rights in marital, familial, social, educational, economic and political fields. They were assigned a subordinate status. The marriage ideals, power and authority exercised by the joint family and caste system, combined with illiteracy, age old traditions, seclusion within the four walls of the house, made it difficult for them to seek fuller personality development. They had scant personal identity and few rights.[63]

Cousin, referring to the status of women at the end of the 19th century, states that the condition of women was at its lowest point of literacy, of individuality, of health, of social status, of freedom of movement, of initiative and of economic status.[64]

According to Dube, this deterioration in the status of women brought about a number of consequences. To quote his own words,

> with these changes in the status of women, it was inevitable that their character and personalities should also be affected. The uneducated were considered on a level with *Sudras*, married before their characters were fully developed, transferred from the loving and sympathetic atmosphere of the parent's house to the house of the parents-in-law where an atmosphere of awe prevailed apprehensive of suppression frequently

> forced to drag on a miserable existence in an interminable widowhood. Their character suffered from forced repression in some directions and unnatural stimulation in other. They had no status in society, none in their own estimation. They were more like puppets which move when someone else pulls the strings than individual human beings with minds of their own.[65]

The reasons that are responsible for the deterioration of the status of women in India were: (i) patriarchal joint family system, (ii) polygamy and the *sati* customs, (iii) enforced widowhood, denial of the right to divorce and right to remarry after widowhood, and (iv) child marriage and the *purdah* system. Because of child marriages to much older men, there was an increase in the number of widows. Both child marriage and the *purdah* custom led to low literacy rate among women. Their entry to social, political and religious functions was prohibited. They were depressed to such an extent that they could not comprehend their own freedom and independent personality. During this period one finds exceptional women like Chand Bibi, Jhansi Laxmibai, Ittur Rani Channamma and Rani Abbakka, who made their remarkable impact in the field of administration.[66]

The British were the first rulers who unified the country as a whole and were liberal in their thinking. They believed that rational thinking had to be the basis for all customs and institutions and customs and institutions not based on reason had to be done away with. Hence, during the British rule, Indian society faced significant modifications. The British government worked slowly and succeeded in providing an alternative way of life for those who wanted change, by introducing a new type of economy, state structure, educational system and also by passing new social legislations.

For the upliftment of women in India several factors are responsible. The first one was the direct influence of the British, noted for their courtesy towards women and the second, the general awakening of Asians in the twentieth century. The political struggle for India's independence also gave considerable force to the feminist movement in India.[67]

The position of girls, women and widows improved during British period. The widow was ill-treated by her in-laws and kinsmen as the virtual destroyer of her husband during the British times. She was never allowed to appear cheerful or wear bright clothes or ornaments. She had to drudge along day and night and was the victim of all kinds of insolence by other women of the household including servants. The tragedy became all the more poignant if the widow happened to be a child. Therefore in order to improve her lot, the British passed the Hindu Widows Remarriage Act, 1856. This Act was enacted to remove all the legal barriers to remarriage of Hindu widows. Further, women acquired a new social status because of the new social legislation called the Civil Indian Marriage Act III of 1872.

The incidence of the cruel practice of *sati* was on the increase throughout the 17th and 18th centuries, because at this time religion had become corrupt and people were governed by the priests. It was a stage of Hinduism when people had become strict followers of customs and conventions. People firmly believed that man's sins were completely washed out if his widow was burnt alive with his dead body. The pitiful plight of the widows who were forced to commit *sati* attracted the attention of a good number of enlightened Indians and the British under the leadership of Raja Ram Mohan Roy and Lord William Bentick. In spite of strong opposition, a historic resolution of great importance was passed on December 14, 1929 by which *sati* was made "a crime of culpable homicide punishable with fine, imprisonment or both."

The British introduced female education in India. But the system of child marriage came in the way of the spread of female education. Hence in 1929 they also passed the Child

Marriage Restraint Act. This Act was also amended by the Acts VIII and XIX in 1938 and in 1978. This Act restricted the evils of early marriage and increase in the number of girl widows. The Act not only prohibited the solemnization of child marriages but also raised the minimum age for marriage of girls to 14. Under section 5 of the 1929 Act, the marriage of girls below 14 years and boys below 18 years of age was to be penalized. The 1929 Child Marriage Restraint Act was also known as the *sarda* Act. Besides removing the evils of child marriage, it promoted female education. This led to the improvement in the position of the daughter.

Later, the British realized that they could stop *sati* by police force but that they could not arrange the remarriage of widows. These widows had to suffer because they had no property of their own. To improve the economic condition of the women, the Hindu Women's Right to Property Act of 1937 was passed. According to Section 3 of the Act, on the death of a Hindu male, not only his son would succeed but also his widow and the widow of the son of the deceased. By this Act a widow got the right to claim partition and a right of enjoyment of that property during her life time. Though she was made a limited owner of her husband's property, she was freed from depending on other members of her husband's family for food and other necessary requirements.

The familial social status of the wife also improved during the British period because of the rise of female education and the rise in the age of marriage. The Hindu Women's Right of Separate Residence and Maintenance Act of 1946 enabled Hindu wives to claim maintenance even without having judicial separation under certain circumstances.

Besides these governmental efforts, in 1917 Mrs. Annie Besant tried to promote women's education through the Indian Association. In 1920 the Federation of Universities of women was established and in 1925 the National Council of women started. Great personalities like Raja Ram Mohan

Roy, the founder of Brahma Samaj, Ishwarchandra Vidyasagar, Dayananda Saraswati, the founder of Arya Samaj, Keshub Chandra Sen, Gopal Krishna Gokhale, Ramakrishna Paramahamsa, Swami Vivekananda, Padita Ramabai and others tried to bring out unprecedented awakening among women who were downtrodden and had been oppressed for centuries.

The familial social and legal position of the Hindu women was greatly improved during the British period, as compared to the Muslim period. Although only a small section of women took advantage of these measures and privileges given, their initiation was indeed significant. During India's struggle for independence, thousands of women took part under the leadership of Mahatma Gandhi. Sarojini Naidu, Vijayalakshi Pandit and Kasturba Gandhi were some of the unique women personalities. Gill has rightly observed about the achievements with regard to the status of women during the British period: "If a person who died a hundred years ago came to life today, the first and most important change that would strike him is the revolution in the position of women."[68]

Due to the principles of democracy based on liberty, a woman's role began to change toward greater emancipation from man's domination. The role of wife-mother was affected by this new freedom. In India, due to efforts of social reformers and social legislations, women were brought out of the confines of their homes.[69] The process of industrialization and urbanization had their share in the changes which followed.[70] It was the 20th century that brought about dynamic changes and new concepts which affected the status of women, giving them fresh dignity and importance.

The constitution of the Indian Republic has incorporated in its objectives the principles of equality and has ushered in the Indian womenfolk into a new era. It has also proclaimed the quality of men and women in all domains of life.[71] In Article 15 of the Constitution it is mentioned that 'the state shall not discriminate against any citizen only on the ground of religion, caste, sex, place of birth or any of them' and Article 16 expressly provides, 'there shall be equality of opportunity for all citizens in matters relating to employment or appointment to any office under the State'. Under Articles 325 and 326 women are not only given voting rights but also the right to stand for election. They can take part in the political life of the country and hold any office from the highest to the lowest. Even the Directive Principles of State Policy enumerate certain directives towards the emancipation of women. Article 39 provides 'equal pay for equal work irrespective of sex.' The modern Indian legislations have stabilized the position of women by offering them the same rights, opportunities and openings which men have.

The Hindu Succession Act 1956 has statutorily recognized the right to property of the Hindu daughter. This Act has placed the daughter on a par with the son. Now she can succeed to the undivided interest of her father in the joint property and to the separate property of the father along with other heirs specified in clause one of the schedule. Dowry system, an abominable social evil, which makes young women's life miserable, has been curbed by the enactment of the Dowry Prohibition Act of 1961. Education is also made free and compulsory for all the children of 5-14 age group. Accessibility to education and availability of increasing opportunities for acquiring education has brought about tremendous changes in the role of women.

At present, the wife enjoys respectable position. She can even live separately under section 18 of the Hindu Adoption and Maintenance Act, 1956, and can claim maintenance under certain circumstances. The husband cannot adopt a son or a daughter under Section 7 of the Hindu adoption and Maintenance Act 1956, without the consent of his wife. The wife under section 8 can adopt a son or daughter when her husband has completely and finally renounced the world or has ceased to be a Hindu or has been declared by a court of competent jurisdiction to be of unsound mind. Under the Hindu Marriage Act, 1955 both husband and wife can claim divorce. Further, the Act has provided the wife more grounds, like sodomy or bestiality under section 13(2) to divorce her husband.

Widow Remarriage is legalized under section 14 of the Hindu Succession Act 1956 which made her the absolute owner of property. She is not divested of the property which she has inherited from her first husband even after her remarriage. Section 8 of the Hindu Adoption and Maintenance Act, 1956 empowers her to adopt a son or daughter to herself. Section 6 of the Hindu Minority and Guardianship Act, 1956 recognized her as the natural and legal guardian of her minor children after their father. But the question does not end with the constitutional provisions for male-female equality because constitutional provisions are only the enabling conditions. What is more important is that these rights should be available to women in actual practice. he legislations have to promote emancipation of women to a very large extent. Besides these legislations, under the provision of the Directive Principles of State Policy, each state has undertaken women's welfare programmes. The central and state governments have evinced keen interest in the betterment of the legal, social, educational and cultural status of women. There is hardly any field today wherein women have not entered.

But one or two women do not change the whole system. Legal and constitutional provisions were not enough to shake a long-standing system. It is still a bitter truth and a bleak reality that Indian women have not yet come out of the shackles of the womanhood attire imposed successfully on them by men. Gender biased laws are still prevalent. Women are still deprived of their rights. The society still does not permit women to perform the ritual of death ceremony (*sraddha*). The Hindu culture still limits women's religious rights. Indian women are still within the boundaries of their social and cultural heritage. The 'Lakshman-Rekhas' still confines Hindu women.

India is considered a country of male chauvinism. Male chauvinism has been taken so much for granted throughout the entire course of human and social evolution that no one even raises the question of the position of men in any particular society. It needs a brilliant perspective and acute mind such as that of Betrand Russell to point out the steady deterioration of the male role in modern society, since almost all his functions have been taken over by the state. In contrast, the question of the position of women in any society is one that is often asked. Most veiled is it in the case of these societies which have just emerged from the feudal stage of social development in a sense. The UNO can be said to have put another nail in the coffin of male superiority by declaring 1975 as the International Women's Year, thereby attracting even more notice towards the status of women in present day society, a question that men would prefer to hush up. The justification of the UN decision lies obviously in the fact that women are still treated as more-or-less second class citizens in respect of many democratic rights. They have yet to taste real equality though of course isolated examples of women who have won a place for themselves in their society can be cited. Notably the names of Mrs. Indira Gandhi in India, Mrs. Thatcher in Britain, Mrs. Bandarnaike in Sri Lanka spring to one's mind. Not only have they demonstrated their equality with men, they have in fact established that women can prove more capable, given the opportunity. There are also examples of some societies like the tribal communities of Meghalaya which are regarded as matrilineal where women are held in high esteem, where there is no dowry system. Moreover, it is the groom's prerogative to offer gifts to the bride. Therefore, dowry, bride burning, dowry death and female infanticide are alien phenomenon among them. Under this system, it is the groom that leaves his father's house and shift to the bride's house after the nuptial knot. Another striking feature of the Khasi tribal society of Meghalaya is that there is no illegitimate children under their social system as the children of Khasi clans inherit their mother's title and not that of the father. Therefore, children born out of wedlock are not looked down upon. Nevertheless, exception proves the rule. One finds even today in Britain that female employees are paid less than their male counterparts for the same work. In some countries, certain professions are practically closed to them for example that of the astronauts, though a Russian woman has circled the globe. It is pointed out that male superiority is no longer valid since science has revolutionized man's working and living environment so much that the old considerations do not apply. Now that most arduous tasks requiring tremendous physical energy can be performed by machines which can be operated by pushing a button, differentiations on the basis of physical strength are meaningless. A woman is quite as capable of dealing with the normal situations of life as any man. The fact that she can be raped by a criminal does not invalidate the argument since a man can also be killed or badly mauled by a lunatic. Besides, women do not develop muscles, because they are never allowed to do so. Behavioural psychologists opine that a woman's delicacy and gentleness are a matter of upbringing rather than a question of natural endowment, a fact easily born out by the strength of rural women almost anywhere, but more particularly in countries like India, where wives labour quite as much as their husbands, even at such purely physical tasks as farming. Thus the male really has no justification for the air of superiority he puts on so thoughtlessly.

Unfortunately, whenever an educated and urbanized person thinks about the status of women, he is inclined to visualize the smart, trim, young things seen jaunting around our westernized metropolises and on the basis of this conception to argue that our women have advanced tremendously. Nothing could be farther from the truth. The so called Indian women live in India's villages, and although she has almost outlived the Sita image of her predecessors, she has yet to attain, the kind of liberty depicted so fatuously in our films. And herein we have fine examples of the phenomenon of cultural tag. In layman's terms, this concept means that cultural change invariably lags behind scientific, technological, economic and political changes that take place in a society emerging from feudalism into modern industrialized society. One could also put it in even more prosaic terms by saying that old habits especially cultural traits die hard. On the technological side we may have achieved a fairly rapid transition from the bullock cart stage to the jumbo jet stage, form the hammer and chisel stage to the later stage, from the simply postal delivery stage to the stage of telex messages but our mental predictions have yet to emerge from the cocoon of feudal attitudes. Male superiority is a doctrine one can question only at the risk of inviting trouble and in fact, one wonders who should like to question, because women themselves accept it. For them their husband is still the local representative or at least the immediate representative of God whose will can neither be challenged nor repudiated.

Rural life has undergone certain changes due to the impact of mechanized agriculture, but for the women, life is still the same round of menial tasks aimed at procuring, the maximum comfort for the male members of the family. Even today, she continues to place the same subordinate role, since all major decisions are made by the husband, the father or even the brother. Girls are married of after a mere pretence at obtaining their approval of the prospective bridegroom. In most cases it is presumed that the boy has the right to reject a girl but the reciprocal principle does not hold true. To a great extent, religious notions still govern the lives of a large majority of our countrymen and women, especially the latter. We find more women at a religious gathering than we find men. It is more natural, then, that the old religious, social and cultural taboos, should still dominate a women's life, circumscribe her sphere of movement and deny her that equality that her urban counterparts have won for themselves. Even for the latter, the quality that they have obtained is hardly of their own making. It is the economic factor which has compelled many a husbands to accept the idea of their wife seeking employment to augment the family income. In other cases, it is the force of boredom seeking alleviation that drives young girls to seek careers since otherwise they cannot inject any meaning and purpose into their lives after they have completed the normal course of formal education. A job is one useful way of marking time before being disposed of in the marriage market.

In India's case then, the status of women in modern society has been determined not by the constitutional guarantees or the spate of legislative measures designed to protect their interests but by the social, cultural and economic environment in which they live. If we imagine that a single legislative act can wipe out an entire tradition built upon over hundreds of years, one is sadly mistaken. Untouchability is a crime under our constitution and yet we see it being practised everyday. Demanding dowry is a crime, but it is demanded and obtained throughout the year. Law can and should be an agent and instrument of social change, but its impact unfolds itself gradually as the old and set patters of behaviour gives way under its impact. Making something a crime under the law is not enough to prevent its occurrence. Murder has been considered a crime for centuries and murders occur with increasing frequency today. Similarly there are many examples of crimes against women even today.

It is strange but true that in spite of all the constitutional guarantees, the torture and murder of females continues even before their birth and makes them deprived of their right to life. Amniocentesis, the miraculous way of finding the sex of fetus, has brought a havoc in those areas of the country where this facility is available in the country. This issues is central to the puzzle of 'missing girls'.

In spite of all hardships, Indian womenfolk are optimistic about the light shining out of darkness and struggle hard to enlighten all facets of their personality to create a specific identity in the coming days.

REFERENCES

1. K. Gill, *Hindu Women's Property in India* (New Delhi: Deep and Deep Publications, 1986) p.17
2. As quoted by A.S. Altekar, *The Position of Women in Hindu Civilization* (Delhi: Motilal Banarsidass, 2nd Edn., 1983) p.319
3. P. N. Majumdar, *Races and Cultures of India* (New Delhi: Asia Publishing House, n.y) p.206
4. P. Prabhu, *Hindu Social Organisation* (Bombay: Popular Book Depot, 1958) p.22
5. Y.B. Singh, *Social Life in Ancient India* (New Delhi: Life and Light Publishers, 1981) p.75
6. M. Cormack, *She Who Rides a Peacock : Indian Students and Social Change* (Bombay: Asia Publishing House, 1961) p.104
7. N. Gorwaney, *Self Image and Social Change : A Study of Female Students* (New Delhi: Sterling Publishers,) p.2
8. R. Mehta, *The Western Educated Hindu Women* (Bombay: Asia Publishing House, 1970) p.16 and 113
9. G. Sudha, "Changing Status of Women in Society," *Women : Her Problems and Her Achievements*, ed., Sarojni Shintri, (Dharwad: Karnatak University, 1977) p.91
10. *Atharva Veda*, VI, 2-3
11. B. S. Upadhyaya, *Women in Rigveda* (New Delhi: S. Chand and Co., 1974) p.43

12. *Ibid.*, pp.44-46
13. A. S. Altekar, p.338
14. Radha Binod Pal, *The History of Hindu Law* (Calcutta: University of Calcutta, 1958) p.302
15. M. N. Banerjee, "Hindu Family and Freudian Theory," *Indian Journal of Social Work*, 1944-45, pp.180-86
16. Shakuntala Rao Shastri, Women in the Vedic Age, 3rd edn. (Bombay: Baratiya Vidya Bhavan, 1960) pp.4-5
17. *Rigveda*, II.17
18. *Rigveda*, III.31-32
19. Radha Binod Pal, p.45
20. A.S. Altekar, pp.338-39
21. K. Gill, p.23
22. Venkatarayappa, *Feminine Roles* (Bombay: Popular Prakashan, 1966) pp.36-37
23. A.S. Altekar, pp.144-45
24. *Ibid.*, p.118
25. Shakuntala Rao Shastri, pp.23-24
26. A.S. Altekar, p.340
27. K. Gill, p.26
28. *Gautama Samhita*, II.9.24
29. *Vasistha Samhita*, XVII.70-71
30. A.S. Altekar, p.345
31. *Brihaspati*, XXV.56
32. *Manu Smriti*, IX.118
33. *Yajnavalkya Smriti*, II.115
34. A.S. Altekar, p.345
35. *Ibid.*, p.348
36. *Yajnavalkya Smriti*, II.115
37. *Ibid.*, II.148
38. *Mahabharat*, XIII, 55.7
39. A.S. Altekar, pp.146-149
40. *Manu Smriti*, V.157, 158, 160
41. A. S. Altekar, p.353

42. R. Chaudhary, "Status and Role of Women : Great Indian Women through the Ages," *Role and Status of Women in Indian Society* (Calcutta: Firma KLM, 1978) p.31
43. Chandrakala Hate, *Changing Status of Women* (Bombay: Allied Publishers, 1969) p.173
44. J. A. Abbe Dubois, *Hindu Manners, Customs and Ceremonies*, trans. H. Beauchampa, 3rd edn. (n.place: OUP, 1906) p.357
45. Ila Mukherjee, *Social Status of North Indian Women* (Agra: Shivala Aggarwal and Co., 1972) pp.114-135
46. Chandrakala Hate, p.175
47. S. Sridevi, *Century of Indian Womanhood* (Mysore: Rao and Raghva Co., 1965) p.75
48. Banerjee, p.184
49. Brabara Ward, *Women in the New Asia* (New York: UNESCO, 1963) p.102
50. Misra Rekha, *Women in Mughal India* (Delhi: Oriental Publisher, 1957) p.132
51. Tara Ali Baig, *Women of India* (Delhi: Government of India Publications, 1958) p.12
52. K. Gill, p.34
53. A.S. Altekar, p.156
54. I. B. Horner, *Women Under Primitive Buddhism* (Varanasi: Motilal Banarsidass, 1975) p.73
55. P.V. Kare, *History of Dharmashastras II* (Poona: Bhandarkar Oriental Research Institute, 1955) p.587
56. Vedavyasa I, 53
57. Henry Maine, *Early History of Institutions* (London: John Murray, 1934) p.335
58. J. A. Abbe, Dubois, pp.357-58
59. A. S. Altekar, p.130
60. P. V. Kare, p.635
61. Tara Ali Baig, p.12
62. Basu Krishna, "Movement for Emanicpatio of Women in the 19th Century," *Role and Status of Women in Indian Society* (Calcutta: Firma KLM, 1978) p.38

63. A. De'Souza, *Women in Contemporary India* (Delhi: Manohar Publications, 1975) pp.79-81
64. Cousin Margret E., *Indian Womanhood Today* (Allahabad: Kitabistan, 1947) p.13
65. S.C. Dube, "Mah'r and Women's Role in India: A Sociological Review," ed. Barbara Ward, *Women in the New Asia*, p.196
66. G. Sudha, p.90
67. K. Gill, p.35
68. *Ibid.*, p.38
69. B. Kuppuswamy, *Social Change in India* (Delhi: Vikas Publishing House, 1972) p.84
70. Ailen D. Ross, *The Hindu Family in the Urban Setting* (London: Oxford University Press, 1961) p.117
71. Tara Ali, p.32

4

Rights of Women

In this chapter, I deal with the concepts of right, human rights and women's rights and the system of women's rights in India and the world.

All rights are generally classified into two categories: natural and conventional. Natural rights are those rights which are believed to be possessed by both men and women by virtue of their nature of humanity, whereas conventional rights are acquired by virtue of contract or ownership. Between these, natural rights are considered more fundamental. Natural rights are universal rights. Everyone holds them irrespective of caste, colour, creed, sex, religion and culture. But conventional rights are specific rights they vary from one context to another according to cultural conventions and circumstances etc. The natural rights theorists believe that natural rights are derived from the very nature of a human being. Theological rights theorists believe that natural rights are accorded by the divine being, God. Others believe no ground can be give for natural rights since they are self-evident. But whatever the case might be, the concepts of right, natural rights, human rights and women's rights require philosophical analysis.

To gain philosophical clarity on the notion of right, let us consider the notion according to John Locke (1632-1704) mainly but with a few scanty references to certain other philosophers as well. Locke, the Englishman, was the theoretical progenitor of democracy as it is practiced world over today. His *Second Treatise on Civil Government* was inspirational to the founders of modern America and the non-monarchical France. In the theory and practice of politics, Locke was directly opposed to Hobbes, the earlier Englishman, whose notion of right was closely connected to his notion of government and civil rule. According to Locke, and rightly so, men live amicably on the whole. He calls life in general as life in a 'state of nature.' Unlike the picture of life in general that Hobbes painted, Locke rightly saw that men lived largely in peace, were not necessarily egoistic, though sometimes they acted selfishly, owned private property and disposed it off at will etc. More importantly, Locke believed in the equality of all men in the state of nature, for he says:

> A state also of equality, wherein all the power and jurisdiction is reciprocal, no one having more than another; there being nothing more evident than that creatures of the same species and rank, promiscuously born to all the same advantages of nature, and the use of the same faculties, should also be equal one amongst another without subordination or subjection...[1]

However, even in the state of nature, men are bound by the 'law of nature' in order to make everyone's freedom count. The 'law of nature' is: "...being all equal and independent, no one ought to harm another in his life, health, liberty, or possessions..."[2] Since men also tend to transgress the law of nature sometimes, the injured party has the right to punish the transgressor. But in the case of punishment there may be grave injustice done unto the victim if punishments could be meted out capriciously. Hence, the need to form societies, rule of law and a civil government, which in short is democracy. Locke says:

> And thus the commonwealth comes by a power to set down what punishment shall belong to the several

> transgressions which they think worthy of it, committed amongst the members of that society, (which is the power of making laws) as well as it has the power to punish any injury done unto any of its members, by anyone that is not of it, (which is the power of war and peace:) and all this for the preservation of the property of all the members of that society, as far as possible.[3]

Locke also speaks of the 'state of war' which is the opposite of the 'state of nature.' In the state of war, one or a group claims absolute dominion over others, leading to a struggle for survival. Locke's ready example for the state of war is monarchical rule of subjugation of the citizenry. Here the principle of equality is seriously undermined and governance is carried out by capricious decree. But the state of war is not the common picture as Hobbes thought. It is, instead, an exception to the general rule for Locke.

Now, whereas the government has the power (i) to administer law impartially (judiciary), (ii) to enforce the law when broken (executive), and (iii) to lay down laws consistently and uniformly (legislature), there are also certain areas of human conduct into which the government cannot interfere. Here comes John Locke's famous doctrine of rights, which is believed to be the predecessor of the celebrated Bill of Rights in the American Constitution. Some of these rights into which the government cannot interfere in the American Constitution are the right to freedom of expression, of worship etc., but according to the author of the theory of rights, Locke, the most important of these is the right to own and dispose off private property. Let us consider below his own words in this regard:

> The great and chief end, therefore, of men's uniting into commonwealths, and putting themselves under government, is the preservation of their property...
>
> The great end of men's entering into society being the enjoyment of their properties in peace and safety, and the great instrument and means of that being the laws

> established in that society; the first and fundamental positive law of all commonwealths is the establishing of the legislative power; as the first and fundamental natural law, which is to govern even the legislative itself, is the preservation of the society...
>
> ... the supreme power cannot take from any man part of his property without his own consent: for the preservation of property being the end of government, and that for which men enter into society, it necessarily supposes and requires, that the people should have property, without which they must be supposed to lose that, by entering into society, which was the end for which they entered into it; too gross an absurdity for any man to own.[4]

However, Locke means by 'private property' not only a man's possessions but also his life and liberties. He does not make clear distinctions between these. One should not be deprived of one's properties because it is a fruit of one's labour to a large extent and in a sense part of a person is invested in his property.

Locke's notion of natural right in general and the right to private property in particular is in sharp contrast to that of Thomas Hobbes (1588-1679), another renowned Englishman, and that of the distinguished Frenchman Jean-Jacques Rousseau (1712-1778). Hobbes, Locke's earlier countryman, did not in the least believe in the right to property of individuals. For him property is a creation of society and in the state of nature there is no such thing as private property. What one can gather and keep by force one does own and there is no such thing as a 'right' to own property, according to Hobbes. Hobbes, as is well-known, lived in a most unsettled time in England, and probably deriving from his experiences, supported the need for a firmly set monarchical rule. For this he based his views on a theory of human nature, in which men are pictured as constantly in a state of war, in which there is "no arts; not letters; no society; and which is worst of all, continual fear, and danger of violent death; and the life of man, solitary, poor, nasty, brutish, and short."[5] In this utterly selfish state of pure nature, Hobbes thought 'every man has a right to everything'[6] which could conversely be that no man had a right to anything because everyone had equal right to everything and there was no power to curtail or grant a right. Today, after centuries of monarchical and right and left wing autocratic excesses, it is not difficult to show conclusively how Hobbes' views were seriously flawed and defeatist. His psychological theory of human nature too is erroneous since as a matter of fact men are not always egoistic but are often altruistic as well. For Hobbes, the political ideal is to surrender one's rights to the sovereign whether a monarch or a collective. This was not a grave difficulty for Hobbes as for him there were no natural rights but all rights were contractual, which could be transferred as easily as they were contracted to a sovereign.

Rousseau, on the other hand, while agreeing with Hobbes that there are no natural rights, disagreed with Hobbes' conclusions from that premise. He thought that men in the state of nature did not have any natural rights but they therefore did not behave necessarily and always selfishly. He says:

> Hobbes had seen clearly the defects of all the modern definitions of natural right: but the consequences which he deduces from his own show that he understands it in an equally false sense... savages (men in the state of nature) are not bad merely because they do not know what it is to be good: for it is neither the development of the understanding nor the restraint of law that hinders them from doing ill; but the peacefulness of their passions, and their ignorance of vice.[7]

Unlike Locke, Rousseau believed that before the formation of society there was neither mine nor thine and no true conception of justice; the question was merely one of subsistence. The social contract is signed for the reason of defending and protecting the persons and possessions of each one who has entered into the compact. The social order thus created is for the sake of order and this social order, though sacred, does not come from nature but from conventions. Rousseau also did not believe in any natural equality of all men but an equality created on the basis of a contract. He says: "... instead of destroying natural inequality, the fundamental compact substitutes, for such physical inequality as nature may have set up between men, an equality that is moral and legitimate, and that men, who may be unequal in strength or intelligence, become every one equal by convention and legal right."[8]

Coming back to Locke, no doubt, Locke's best known contributions are towards the concept of democracy but his theory of rights is enshrined in the doctrine of civil government. Locke believed that a democratic form of government is the only type of government that could guarantee individuals their rights. He also believed that by nature, that is, before allowing the formation of society or government, man is already endowed with certain rights. They are not given to him by the society/ government and so it has no power to take it away from him. The more modern notion of 'equality of all before law' is a derivation from Locke's doctrine of rights. Locke realized that if the formation of society, government and the rule of law (the giving and taking of rights) is made a contractual affair, then the doctrine of rights had to be based on feeble grounds. Instead if it is founded on the very nature of the human person (concept of natural rights), then it becomes an obligation that every owes to everyone else by virtue of being human.

John Locke's theory of government, despite being an original and excellent contribution of concretized thought, has been criticized as a promotion of the rule of the majority. The critic, however, should know that Locke was on the side of the rule of the people and not of a few or one. The error he made of not making provisions for the protection of the minorities in his theory of government was well rectified by Locke's great critic, John Stuart Mill. More close to our concern here, his theory of rights is criticized on the ground that his claim of the existence of rights in the state of nature before the formation of government is invalid since there is no government to grant the rights in that state. The theory of natural rights is criticized on many other grounds as well, about which we will deal later. Again, it is also argued that certain freedoms like the freedom of speech or the freedom to own private property cannot be absolute, since these might at times act as a hindrance towards the public good, which is also a fundamental duty of a government to work towards. Hence, more moderate advocates of the theory of rights tend to abandon Locke's view of 'absolute rights' and say that 'right' is a matter of degree. They can be sometimes suspended or infringed with majority consent when the public welfare is genuinely at stake.

The question 'whether there are any natural rights?' has to be discussed a bit further to have a better understanding of the concept of right. In fact, the concepts of human rights and women's rights are based on a conception of natural rights. Of course, there are various types of rights. According to Immanuel Kant (1724-1804), natural right is that right which rests upon pure rational principles *a priori* and positive or statutory right is what proceeds from the will of a legislator. Again, an innate right for Kant is that right which belongs to everyone by nature and an acquired right is that right which is founded upon juridical acts. Kant was a firm believer in the innate freedom of the individual and so in the right of each person as person to be his own master by right. In line with his famous categorical imperative, Kant's formulation of the universal principle of right reads: "Act externally in such a manner that the free exercise of thy will may be able to co-exist with the freedom of all others, according to a universal law."[9] However, Kant believed that possessing something, say private property, was not a natural/innate right but an acquired right. Freedom "in so far as it can co-exist with the freedom of all according to a universal law, it is the one sole original, inborn right belonging to every man in virtue of his humanity."[10]

I quote rather extensively from Ralph Mason Blake to show what nature natural rights possess:

> The traditional conception of "natural" rights, whatever its other content, seems at least always to be that of a system of "rights" having a deeper and more fundamental character than any merely legal rights, of a system of rights possessing an ultimate and objective validity not derived from their relation to any system of positive law. Natural rights, as their name indicates, are supposed to be based instead upon a law of nature itself, independent of any positive enactments of men, and of a higher validity. It is therefore considered possible to contrast merely legal rights with natural rights in case of conflict to assert the superior claims of the latter. Just as positive rights are derived from positive laws and correlated with legal duties, so natural rights are conceived to be based upon the "natural law," prescribed by the very nature of things, and to be correlated with certain natural duties. And, like legal rights, natural rights appear usually in the form of *claims*, often to some freedom, immunity, or, privilege, made legitimate by this "law of nature."...
>
> ... "natural laws," so far as they are to define natural rights, must be principles of permanent, and not of merely transitory, validity, and furthermore that they must be such as are valid for all men everywhere. In other words, the truly natural rights must be those claims, liberties, and privileges the possession of which by the person or persons in question will continue, so long at least as human nature and the laws of the physical universe remain substantially what they now are, to constitute permanent and general conditions of human happiness.[11]

In the above sense, I believe, there are certain natural

rights for humans. However, it is today keenly contested whether there are such rights. Many writers, for instance, those with a utilitarian bend of mind, strongly disagree to the proposition that there are in fact such rights. Nevertheless, even Utilitarians try to reconcile their moral theory with the natural rights of humans. To say the least, it is a belief in the natural rights of persons by virtue of their being humans that the famous Universal Declaration of Human Rights of the United Nations, adopted in 1948, is formulated. Several articles of this sacred declaration speak of the assumption of natural rights. Its first article says: "All human beings are born free and equal in dignity and rights. They are endowed with reason and conscience and should act towards one another in a spirit of brotherhood."[12] Its preamble has the following clauses:

> Whereas recognition of the inherent dignity and of the equal and inalienable rights of all members of the human family is the foundation of freedom, justice and peace in the world, ... Whereas the peoples of the United Nations have in the Charter reaffirmed their faith in fundamental human rights, in the dignity and worth of the human person and in the equal rights of men and women and have determined to promote social progress and better standards of life in larger freedom, ...[13]

Similarly, constitutions of democracies all over the world are based on the assumption of natural human rights.

How can we defend the existence of natural rights? One way of defending, one that was followed by John Locke in the *Second Treatise on Civil Government*, is to defend them on the foundation of God, the creator. Such defence of natural rights has fallen into disfavour, especially because of the decreasing influence of religion and the increasingly prevalent atmosphere of secularism. Another is the foundation that St. Thomas Aquinas provided on the basis of natural law ethics, which again has several loose ends because of its claim that humans have inbuilt inclinations to attain their natural ends and that the natural rights are evident from these purposes of man. However, the most commonly used defence for natural rights is the claim that they follow from a reflection on human personhood itself.[14]

Hence, despite many arguments to the contrary, I would like to base myself here on the existence of natural human rights. There are certain general features of humans which are lasting features of their nature. This being the case, there are also certain general and permanent conditions for the attainment of values, which we call natural rights of humans.

Now I come to what are called women's rights. It should be remembered that in the political theory of rights of John Locke, for instance, there was no place for women. However, humanity has taken great strides since Locke's times and today whatever Locke and the authors of the American Declaration of Independence, the Bill of Rights in the American Constitution and the French Declaration of the Rights of Man and of the Citizen had said imply not just the male sex. However, recognition of women's rights, even the basic political right of women's suffrage, was a hard fought achievement. In the United States, women's suffrage was granted through the 19th Amendment to the U.S. Constitution only in 1920. In Great Britain, though the Parliament enfranchised women householders, householders' wives and women university graduates over 30 years of age, complete political equality of British women with their men counterparts was achieved only as late as in 1928. New Zealand was the first to grant women's suffrage in 1893. The other countries which granted women's suffrage before the United States were: Australia (1902); Finland (1906); Norway (1913); Denmark (1915); the Netherlands and the Soviet Union (1917); Canada and Luxembourg (1918); Austria, Czechoslovakia (now the Czech Republic and Slovakia), Germany, Poland, and Sweden (1919). Besides, the Universal Declaration of Human Rights of the United Nations recognized the equality of the sexes in 1948 by saying, as quoted above, in the Preamble that the people of the United Nations have reaffirmed their faith in fundamental human rights, in the dignity and worth of the human person and *in the equal rights of men and women.*

Let us first consider what 'human rights' are. There are several definitions of 'human right' and one of the oldest is given in the American Declaration of Independence: 'We hold these truths to be self-evident, that all men are created equal, that they are endowed by their Creator with certain unalienable Rights, that among these are Life, Liberty, and the pursuit of Happiness.' The rights described in the 30 articles of the Universal Declaration of Human Rights include the right to life, liberty, and security of person; to freedom of conscience, religion, opinion, expression, association, and assembly; to freedom from arbitrary arrest; to a fair and impartial trial; to freedom from interference in privacy, home, or correspondence; to a nationality; to a secure society and an adequate standard of living; to education; and to rest and leisure. The declaration also affirms the rights of every person to own property; to be presumed innocent until proven guilty; to travel from a home country at will and return at will; to work under favorable conditions, receive equal pay for equal work, and join labor unions at will; to marry and raise a family; and to participate in government and in the social life of the community. According to McCloskey, most of these rights in the Universal Declaration are derivative rights from basic self-evident human rights which include "the rights to life, health, and to bodily integrity; to respect as persons, and hence to respect for one's moral autonomy and integrity and a possessor of feelings, creative imagination, and needs of many kinds; to self-development and to education as a condition and element thereof; to access to knowledge and truths."[15]

All women's rights are human rights as the Fourth United Nations World Conference on Women at Beijing in 1995 rightly said:

> All human rights – civil, cultural, economic, political and social, including the right to development – are universal, indivisible, interdependent and interrelated . . . the human rights of women and the girl-child are an inalienable, integral and indivisible part of universal human rights. The full and equal enjoyment of all human rights and fundamental freedoms by women and girls is a priority for governments and the United Nations and is essential for the advancement of women.[16]

However, a distinction may be made between women's human rights in general and women's rights in particular. 'Women's human rights' in general signifies all those rights which women possess in virtue of their being human. For instance, all human rights violations where women happen to be victims like persecution of politically active women, discrimination against members of an ethnic community, forced evictions etc. These violations, in short, are not gender specific. 'Women's rights' in narrower sense signifies those rights which are gender specific. For instance, violations of women's rights are gender specific violations suffered only or predominantly by women like rape, forced prostitution, trafficking in women, discrimination in nationality laws etc. Hence, while all women's rights are human rights, all human rights are not women's rights. However, it must be admitted here that it becomes often difficult to ascertain whether some right is a women's human right or a women's gender right. For instance, even when there is persecution of a woman on account of her political activities, the form of the violation may be influenced by her sex.[17]

One might ask why women have been denied their rights and their due share for centuries before they began to fight for towards the beginning of the twentieth century. There are several answers to this question, and some of them I have already dealt with in the preceding chapters. But I would like to answer the above question from a feminist point of view. From a feminist perspective, the perpetration of the subjugation of women had been made possible by the social intricacies of patriarchy, a complex social order in which all authority and power are vested with *pater* or father or the male member(s) of the family and the society in general. Under this system both political and familial orders are male-oriented and male-ruled. "A society is considered patriarchal when men establish or inherit a social order where they dominate positions of power and authority or when important achievements and historical events are attributed to the actions of men."[18] Patriarchal social orders have been set up not only in the smallest of social setups like the family or the widest like the political unit of, say, a nation. It was also the case in religious orders like Christianity or Hinduism. In the Roman Catholic Church, the biggest of the many Christian denominations, it is believed that God the Father has directly extended His authority to the bishops of the Church. In fact, the early bishops of the Church are called the 'patriarchs'. Catholic Church, hence, does not believe in ordaining women to the priesthood, which is the centre of authority in the Church. In the Hindu religious and social order of India only men inherited property and they dominated political, familial and religious power. Politically most societies believed in the divine right of kings to rule the society. Even when more democratic political organizations, which were hugely revolutionary in their day, were set up, they were still conceived as male-dominated. When the famous U.S Declaration of Independence came into effect, those behind it were all men and those who signed the first Constitution of that modern and very revolutionary state were called the 'founding fathers.' Religion controlled the affairs of men and women before the days of the Enlightenment so strongly that any custom or convention having a religious sanction was considered sacrosanct and the breaking of it almost ostracized the transgressing party. During such times religious sanction was readily granted to a male-centred patriarchal social order. In several chapters of this book I dwell at length on how the Hindu religious order of India promoted a patriarchal social order. Similarly Christianity and Islam, two major world religions, have been staunch promoters of patriarchy. Such religions promoted the religious sanction and rationale that male dominance was the natural or God-given order of the society.[19] However, in our times a lot of feminist deconstruction of scripture, ancient texts of history and society and even customs and conventions has shown how religious and other important customs of social interactions, written and unwritten, were carefully tailored to suit men and their machismo. One such work, outstanding and trailblazing in its own right, was *The Second Sex* (1949) of Simone de Beauvoir (1908-1986) one of the most important feminist theorist of the existentialist tradition in philosophy that emphasized individual freedom and choice, besides being perhaps the most prominent woman philosopher of the 20th century, novelist, playwright, autobiographer and essayist. *The Second Sex* is an analysis of women's existential situation in the world and their hope for liberation. Like all existentialists, De Beauvoir also said that individuality is not a determination of one's birth and allied circumstances or by any pre-given nature but a construction, very special and complex, that the free individual makes after her birth in a meaningless and harsh world. Existential philosophy of the individual was de Beauvoir's first step also to her feminist analysis of woman in *The Second Sex*.

> Analyzing history, literature, and myth, de Beauvoir argued that Western culture established oppositional gender associations based on the primacy of men. In these gender types, for example, men are assumed to be intellectual, while women are instinctual; men are

> superior, while women are inferior. De Beauvoir asserted that the very idea of individual self is associated in Western culture with men; women, she maintained, borrowing a term from existentialism, are the *Other*—alien, always less than men. Unless women liberated themselves from these associations, maintained in institutions such as schools and churches, they could never achieve full individual identity. *The Second Sex* was an important stimulus to the feminist movement that grew in the 1960s and 1970s, and it remains one of the most compelling applications of existentialist philosophy to social and cultural problems.[20]

De Beauvoir says in *The Second Sex*: "One is not born, but rather becomes, a woman. No biological, psychological or economic fact determines the figure that the human female presents in society; it is civilization as a whole that produces this creature ... which is described as feminine."[21]

Hence, though patriarchal social order was the general reason for the weakening of the position of women all over the world, several particular reasons may be pointed out within such orders. In patriarchal societies males attributes are attached to heads of families and political units like machismo, overtly aggressive behaviour, valour and muscle power. Such attributes were, however, not mere characterizations but their enactment in whatever form helped males to sustain their power, control, authority and positions. It is well-known that in such a social system several rights were withheld from women and several sanctions and even cruel practices were imposed on them. Withholding of rights was done under the assumption that women were inferior in the use of the faculty of reason, God had ordained them so and that they were physically and psychologically weaker than men, needing protection and support rather than equal treatment. This assumption has been challenged with scientific support with the advent of the feminist movement. It has been successfully shown that women's supposed inferiority is a social construct and that their supposedly secondary role in society is due to socio-cultural conditioning.

In the world over, women's fight to get their rights was a tedious and often difficult task. The main reason for this was a carefully ingrained attitudinal structure and theory that promoted male-domination in almost every sphere of life. Sir Robert Filmer, an influential English political scientist of the 17th century, for example, held that political and social submission to the males is a natural condition as all authority can be traced back to the first man, Adam, in whom was vested all power by God, the Creator. It was John Locke who later in the same century challenged this argument, as Locke was sternly opposed to patriarchal rule in the political arena. He refuted the doctrine of divine right of kings and said that it was the people themselves who should rule themselves through their representatives, a rule which today we call the democracy. But Locke meant only a gender-neutral political rule and not a gender-neutral home and family atmosphere to share power between the spouses. He thought that women submitted themselves to their fathers and to their husbands voluntarily on account of their natural nature. French philosopher and one of the most influential writers of the Enlightenment Period, Rousseau, thought of women as sentimental, frivolous and fit only for being subordinate companion of man. Following Rousseau's attacks on women, the English writer Mary Wollstonecraft wrote *A Vindication of the Rights of Woman* in 1971 defending women's behaviour in society as a corollary of their training, education and upbringing and not on account of any inherent nature. In the next century, Friedrich Engels, German political economist, thought that primitive societies were matriarchies and properties were passed on from mother to daughters. According to Engels, later as civilizations progressed men acquired properties and wanted those to be passed on to their offspring rather than to their women and so sabotaged the rule of women and established patriarchy. Political and social scientists of the twentieth century tried to explain that patriarchy as a form of government came to an end after the Enlightenment with the coming of the notions of liberty and individual freedom. But these theorists did not explain how gender inequalities continued to persist in society. This bafflement was one reason why the women's rights movement met with significant success in that century and thenceforth. Feminists in the recent times believe that patriarchy signified the cultural and social domination of women by men. They also believe that since legal and political equity has already been achieved by women to a significant degree, social attitudes towards women will gradually become positive with time and advocacy strategies. Most feminists believe that attitudes towards women are a socio-cultural construct and so can change. But this change cannot come merely with political and legal actions; social actions at the very family stage should happen before these attitudes change. However, there are also very radical feminists, though few in number, who claim that patriarchy is never going to change and so women should isolate themselves and live separately or obtain very concrete and protective legal and political measures against male violence.[22]

What then are women's rights proper? These are rights that provide equality and equity in the social, economic and political orders for men and women without any reference to their sex. Basically women's rights guard women against sexual/ gender discrimination and they enjoin certain duties as well mainly about how they should treat and respect women. As we stand at the beginning of the 21st century, we can see that women in most parts of the world have gained significant freedom and rights. But this is not a case with some parts of the world. For instance, the radical Islamic regime of the present day Iran has placed severe curtailments on women's rights and freedom. Moreover, whatever legal and political rights women in most parts of the world have so far gained, they still are not complete equals to men in political, economic or social life.

How this can be achieved, nevertheless, is not an area of concern in our enquiry here. I rather propose to enquire into what exactly are some of these rights claimed by women as their rights? I shall consider this both in the international and Indian contexts.

From the international perspective, the United Nations Organization (the UN) has championed women's cause for the past several decades untiringly. The UN has been forming international advocacy groups and organizing international women's conferences with the aim of attaining equality of the sexes. Women have made use of these platforms to raise several of their issues. To take a few examples, a UN organization called the Commission of the Status of Women (CSW) has been a significant contributor to the women's rights efforts made all over the world since 1947. This organization has played significant advocacy roles regarding the status of women and can promote immediate international action in cases of severe women's rights violations. One of the most prominent UN effort was to launch the women's decade (1975-85) in order to concentrate on women's issues on a priority basis. During this period several conferences were organized on themes surrounding equality, development and peace. One of the highlights of the UN women's rights movement is the fourth UN World Conference on women held in Beijing in 1995, which was attended by women delegated from about 200 nations. The Platform for Action created by the Beijing Conference is doing a commendable job in focusing on removing the obstacles to women's participation in the society. Some of the highlights of the Conference on women's rights are the following:

> The World Conference on Human Rights reaffirmed clearly that the human rights of women throughout

> the life cycle are an inalienable, integral and indivisible part of universal human rights...
>
> Every person should be entitled to participate in, contribute to and enjoy cultural, economic, political and social development. In many cases women and girls suffer discrimination in the allocation of economic and social resources. This directly violates their economic, social and cultural rights.
>
> ... reproductive rights rest on the recognition of the basic right of all couples and individuals to decide freely and responsibly the number, spacing and timing of their children and to have the information and means to do so, and the right to attain the highest standard of sexual and reproductive health. It also includes their right to make decisions concerning reproduction free of discrimination, coercion and violence, as expressed in human rights documents.

Violence against women both violates and impairs or nullifies the enjoyment by women of human rights and fundamental freedoms... gender-based violence, such as battering and other domestic violence, sexual abuse, sexual slavery and exploitation, and international trafficking in women and children, forced prostitution and sexual harassment, as well as violence against women, resulting from cultural prejudice, racism and racial discrimination, xenophobia, pornography, ethnic cleansing, armed conflict, foreign occupation, religious and anti-religious extremism and terrorism are incompatible with the dignity and the worth of the human person and must be combated and eliminated. Any harmful aspect of certain traditional, customary or modern practices that violates the rights of women should be prohibited and eliminated...

Many women face additional barriers to the enjoyment of their human rights because of such factors as their race, language, ethnicity, culture, religion, disability or socio-economic class or because they are indigenous people, migrants, including women migrant workers, displaced women or refugees. They may also be disadvantaged and marginalized by a general lack of knowledge and recognition of their human rights as well as by the obstacles they meet in gaining access to information and recourse mechanisms in cases of violation of their rights.[23]

The condition of women vary very significantly even within a country among its various ethnic and religious groups. Though female enfranchisement is achieved in most countries, women's role in running the government and their political role in general is still very insignificant. There are over 100 nations in the world today where there are no female representatives in the government. And ironically, in developed countries the number of women representatives in parliament is less than in developing countries. Though women's legal status is the same as that of men in most parts of the world, about 70 per cent of the world's poor are women. Hence their economic status is still abysmal even after decades of international efforts to have equal workforce of men and women. Of the total labour force in the world, women are less than 35 per cent and their percentage in positions where they can make important decisions is appallingly low, that is, less than five per cent in the world over. In the field of education, women form two-thirds of the world's illiterates, even though enrollment levels at primary level is now nearing the optimum level of equality. Among school dropouts also girls are two-thirds in the world. However, more and more women are today entering into higher education, though not technical education. Regarding reproductive rights in the world, women continue to be too poor to avail the facilities of contraception to gain effective birth control.

Having analysed the concept of 'right', natural right, human rights and women's rights, and briefly the condition of women's rights in the world as a whole, I now come to a somewhat elaborate treatment of women's rights in the country. Here, I must add that an analysis of violation of women's rights will be undertaken in the following chapter and so in this chapter I deal only with a situational and rather critical analysis of the theory and practice of women's rights in India.

In India social and religious life were not looked upon as two separate things until recently when the principle of secularism began to have a greater say in Indian life. Women's position in Indian life was somewhat similar to what it was all over the world. There was a notion of respect for women as mother and faithful wife. There was also the concept of Mother Goddess in Hinduism. However, today from a feminist analysis, it can be clearly seen that most of these notions are carefully knit around providing a very submissive social and familial role for women and a more aggressive, dominant and prominent role to men in society.

Indian classical and cultural texts like the Gita emphasized that wise people treat equally a learned Brahman, an ox, an elephant, a dog and a *shwapaka*, i.e., a member of what was then looked upon as a lower sub-caste.[24] Kautilya, the great political scientist of ancient India, emphasized on the importance of political and other rulers to treat their subjects uniformly.[25]

However, *Manusmriti*, the text that actually came to be practiced in the social life of India, a text that was actually responsible for most of the social customs, proposed the division of human society into two camps of men and women. *Manusmriti* contained the unfortunate proposition that in all stages of her life, woman was to depend upon her father, husband and the son and could not be left to conduct her affairs on her own. Even though this was a very general observation, it actually contained the tacit assumption of the superior capacity of the stronger sex in judging issues and reaching conclusions as to definite action thereon and in implementing decisions. Moreover, *Manusmriti* came to be such a revered text that its injections became sacrosanct and unbreakable. Similarly, Vatsyayana, the great author of Indian classic of sensuality, the *Kamasutra*, assumed that in mundane matters too the male and the female outlooks differed widely. He thought that women were more emotional and prone to express their wishes on impulsive considerations and men were more practical and framed their requirements or objectives after evaluating the facts of the situation.

Given this type of statements in the sacred and learned texts, women in India were looked upon traditionally as more emotional, less practical and rushing into immature and irresponsible conclusions on life's problems than their male counterparts. In their courteous best, these social theorists laid down that the stronger sex was to protect the interests of the weaker sex. That is why in *Manusmriti*'s infamous verse on woman, the verb '*rakshati*' is used to mean 'protect.'

However, Kalidas, the world famous Sanskrit dramatist, is to be singled out for taking a kinder view on women. In two separate occasions Kalidas shows that male judgement was indefensible. In the first context I am referring here from *Abhijnana Shakuntalam*, Shakuntala retorts when Dushyanta makes a sarcastic remark about women in general saying that men arrogantly assume that they are righteous and knowledgeable and that women are devoid of the capacity to reason. Strangely enough, practically all editions of this world renowned drama omit this statement of Shakuntala. In the second context, Kalidas' Sita asks Lakshmana when he told her that Rama had ordered him to take her into the forest away from Ayodhya to be banished whether it was consistent with his training and education to banish her on the ground of mere hearsay even after she had passed the *agni-pariksha* in his presence. In both these contexts Kalidas' progressive views about women are reflected. We need to remember that these views when expressed in those times were starkly revolutionary. However, given such sacred sanction imposed on women, the views of Kalidas had not many takers in those traditional times.

Anti-woman agenda is not confined to India. It is still visibly present even in advanced countries of Europe and America. In India, as for her legal status, woman is no less than man in any sphere of life. Our constitution treats both men and women equally. It may even be said that there are already sufficient laws for the welfare of women, though in most cases women are unaware of their rights in this country.

However, life has not changed with laws being promulgated. Women's workload at home is still huge. In urban areas of India where women go out for employment, men are increasingly sharing the household chores. In cases where this has caused friction within the family and changed the structure of the family from husband-dominance to an egalitarian setup has not been wanting. There are people still who claim that domestic chores are female responsibilities, even if women are employed. In such cases, women's employment has not led to equitable domestic division of labour between the sexes.

In rural areas, where the traditional values have always been so dominant, the contribution of women in agricultural and other economic pursuits has never been recognized. A woman is never considered as an earner for the family unless she has an invalid husband or earns wages through work. Some rural women also face the hurdle of having traditional husbands and in-laws who do not permit them to work outside the family. There is thus a curvilinear relationship between traditions, illiteracy and female work participation in rural areas. Hence, much legislation on the rights of women has not shown real effect because the structure and cultural characteristics of our society did not allow them to bear fruit.

Let us now consider the proprietary rights of women in India in the traditional times. In those times, proprietary rights of women were hardly recognized in any civilization. Women themselves were an item among the movable property of the patriarch. But it was not so in India. Even in the Vedic times the husband and the wife were regarded as the joint owners of the household. The husband was required to take a solemn vow at the time of the marriage that he would never usurp his wife's rights in economic matters. Apastamba construes the joint ownership theory to mean that the wife is entitled to incur the normal expenditure on the household affairs during her husband's absence.[26]

However, Manu does not allow any share to the wife in the property of her husband during his lifetime. She had only the right of maintenance against her husband which could never be denied to her even if she became unchaste or outcaste or persisted in immorality.[27] Another verse also says that a wife, a son and a slave are declared to have no property and the wealth which they earn goes to him to whom they belong.[28] This verse of *Manusmriti* appears to mean simply that the earnings and other receipts of the wife are to go to the husband. It does not indicate anything as to whether or not she is entitled to hold any property by herself as some commentators are prone to suggest.

Stridhana in its origin appeared to have been connected to the custom of bride-price which was greatly denounced by Manu, the law giver. But this custom contributed to the development of the custom of *stridhana*. Owing to their affection for the daughter, the parents gave a part and sometimes even the whole of the bride-price to her to be enjoyed by her as her separate estate during her own lifetime. If she had children, her property would go to them[29] and if not, it would remain with her husband in case of the first five forms of marriage[30] and in case of the other marriages, it would be passed back to her family.[31] Since in some forms of marriage the property of an issueless daughter reverted back to her father, it may be inferred that *stridhana* was actually the bride-price which had been given to her by her father at the time of her marriage. Hence some form of property was given by the father to his daughter also even during those times. There are also scanty references to *stridhana* as gift to the daughter even in the Rgveda.[32]

However, no clear definition of *stridhana* is found in any of the ancient works. Kautilya, however, defines it as the means of subsistence or what could be actually worn on the 'body' of the bride; he fixes the means of subsistence at two thousand *panas* as the maximum while he puts no restriction on what could be given as *avadhya*.[33] Manu, though gives a comprehensive description of *stridhana*, does not define it. According to him, it is of six kinds: what is given before the nuptial fire, what is given on the occasion of the bridal procession, what is given in token of love and what is received from her brother, her mother or her father.[34] But the *Mitaksara* has widened the scope of the *stridhana*. According to it, a property of any description belonging to a woman becomes her *stridhana*, even if it be inherited by her from a male person either as a widow or as a mother.[35] The *Dayabhaga*, on the other hand, observes that a woman can donate, sell or enjoy independently of her husband's control her *stridhana*. According to it, all the gifts from her relations, except any immovable property given to her by the husband himself and also those from others made before the nuptial fire or on the occasion of her departure from her father's house, constitute the *stridhana*. But property inherited by a woman or obtained in partition, gifts from strangers and property acquired by her by means of mechanical arts or by her own labour is not included in her *stridhana*.[36]

But such widening of the scope of the woman's property and her rights over it has not been accepted by any of the commentators of *Manusmriti*. They most probably considered it as wholly inconsistent with the general status of a woman. Henry Maine also seems to think on the same lines:

> The settled property of a married woman incapable of alienation by her husband is well known to the Hindus under the name of *stridhana*. It is certainly a remarkable thing that the institution seems to have

> developed among the Hindus at a period relatively much earlier than among the Romans. But instead of being matured and improved, as it was in Western society, there is reason to think that in the East, under various influences which may partly be traced, it has gradually been reduced to dimensions and importance far inferior to those which at one time belonged to it.[37]

The author shows a deep insight into the Hindu conception of law on this point when he says that except the author of the *Mitaksara* all the commentators who succeeded one another in the schools of Hindu Law show a visibly increasing desire to curtail the proprietary rights of women.

Let us now consider the right of disposal of women of their *stridhana* in the traditional times. Manu says in his usual severity towards women that the wife ought not to spend anything even from her *stridhana* property without her husband's sanction.[38] But the husband could not deprive his wife of the property, except as a temporary disciplinary measure and his relatives could have no share of it during her lifetime. Manu is also silent on whether the husband could make use of his wife's property in times of emergency. Even Kautilya says that women had any such right only in the absence of their husband, and that husband could make use of his wife's property during emergencies only in the first four types of marriages which were socially approved and not in the last four types of marriages.[39] Yajnavalkya lays down that the husband could freely utilize the wife's property in times of dire necessities and he was not required to pay it back.[40] The *Mitaksara* clearly says that except the husband no other person had any right to the woman's property.[41]

Regarding succession to the *stridhana*, the oldest extent text is the *Gautama* which provides that *stridhana* devolves first on the daughter who is unmarried and then on the not so well provided daughter. Kautilya prescribes that if a woman dies during her husband's lifetime, her sons and daughters divide her *stridhana*; if she has no son the daughter alone shares it; or else, the husband takes it.[42] According to Manu, a woman's *stridhana* should be equally shared among her sons and daughters and a share had to be given even to her daughters' daughters.[43] If she had no issue, the property goes to the husband in the first five forms of marriage[44] and in the last three it reverts back to her parents.[45] Yjnavalkya provides that the daughters take the *stridhana* estate of their mother and in their absence it is to devolve upon the male issues and if the woman dies issueless, the husband was entitled to the property in the first four forms of marriage and the woman's parents in the last four forms of marriage.[46]

Upto the 3rd century B.C., the right of the widow to inherit her husband's property was not recognized by any jurist including the Vedic texts, the *Dharmasutras* and the *Baudhayana*. *Apastamba* lays down that in the absence of the son, the property should devolve not upon the widow but upon the nearest male descendant and failing him, it should go to his preceptor and failing him, it should be taken over by a disciple of the deceased to be spent for charitable purposes.[47] A few of the law-givers were inclined to give to the widows the right of maintenance only like Kautilya who says that the widow can maintain her husband's estate if it was taken over by the state.[48] It was Gautama who first came forward to plead for the recognition of the widow's claim to her husband's property. He put forth the proposal that the widow should be regarded as coheir with others who have the claim.[49] Manu too does not recognize the widow as an heir to her sonless husband but gives the claim to the dead man's father, then upon his brother and finally upon a *spinda* and *sakulya* in accordance with his propinquity and when none of these is forthcoming first a preceptor, then a disciple and finally the king should take it over.[50] Such problems arose only when the man died sonless. But even if there was a son, he could not partition the property if one of the parents was alive, though he was the legal heir. This position of Manu has any defence only on moral grounds. But in any case, the widow had no right to her husband's property. The widow was expected to maintain herself from her *stridhana*, for if her husband's property was also vested on her, it also would have to devolve on her daughters after her death. In the course of time, however, the tendency in favour of the recognition of the widow's rights to her husband's property grew stronger. It was felt that she should be the sole heir to her husband's property if he died sonless. This view was for the first time advocated by Vishnu about the beginning of the Christian era. He definitely lays down that in the absence of the sons, the widow shall inherit the whole estate of her husband.[51] Soon after this, Yajnavalkya and Brahaspati[52] joined Vishnu in championing the cause of the widow and gave her the right to succeed to her sonless husband, though writers like Narada[53] and Katyayana[54] did not recognize the right of the widow.

Several positive laws related to women's rights have come about in India after independence. The Equal Remuneration Act, 1976 does not permit wages discrimination between male and female workers. It prescribed the same wages for men and women for the same jobs. The Act also prescribes penalties for those employers who disobey the rules. However, 'equal pay for equal work' is not a fundamental right but only a constitutional goal and an ideal principle (Article 30) mentioned under the Directive Principles of State Policy for making laws. Thus, unlike the fundamental rights, these provisions cannot be enforced by any court.

There has been a steady rise in the number of women taking up jobs since independence. Of the total labour force of 265 million in our country, women constitute nearly 90 million which is about one-third of the total labour force. The employment laws, therefore, give special protection to women employees from harassment or abuse at workplace and from jobs unsuitable to their age or strength. Maternity benefits are provided as one of the social security schemes for women employees. It provides for job security to women during and after pregnancy, leave with full pay and benefits to protect the health of the mother and the baby. It entitles a female worker, having worked for 160 days in a year in the establishment, for six weeks leave during confinement and six weeks after delivery.

The labour laws provide security to workers, including female workers. A female employee cannot be dismissed after charging her with misconduct. At the most, she can be suspended and subsistence allowance has to be paid to her till the enquiry is over. At the inquiry, the employee gets the opportunity to defend herself both by explaining her conduct and by producing witnesses. The dismissed employee is also given an opportunity to appeal to an industrial tribunal or court. Likewise, a retrenched worker is entitled to compensation equivalent to 15 days averâge pay for every year of service. The worker has also to be given one month's notice. During the period of lay-off forced by shortage of raw materials, power, breakdown of machinery and accumulation of stock, an employee is entitled half of the basic wages and dearness allowance. If the lay-off is not bona-fide, a worker can get full wages.

The special Marriage Act, 1954 has permitted girls to select their own life partners if they have attained the age of eighteen years. They can select their mates from outside their own caste, sub-caste, community and religion too, if they so choose. Both boys and girls who want to get married outside their religion and caste can resort to civil marriage which requires no rites or customary ceremonies. Besides providing the minimum age for the civil marriage, the 1954 legislation also lays down three other conditions: neither of the partners has a spouse living, each party must give consent to marriage and the partner should not be a close relative, that is, within the degree of prohibited relationship, unless the custom of their community permits such a marriage. Religious norms and social customs in India had made the marriage of a girl before attaining puberty obligatory. This practice of child marriage persisted in our country till the first quarter of the twentieth century. The special Civil Marriage Act, 1872 had fixed the minimum age of marriage for girls at 14, but this applied only to those girls who married through courts outside their own caste. The Special Marriage Act, 1954 fixed the minimum marriage age at 21 and 18 for boys and girls respectively.

A Hindu marriage was considered to be a *Samskara* and not a contract as it is understood among Muslims. Marriage was, therefore, never permitted to be dissolved except in some lower castes. But, with the advent of education and subsequent attitudinal changes, the ancient law of marriage has been changed. Today marriages are no longer considered in indissoluble. Both the Hindu Marriage Act, 1955 and the Special Marriage Act, 1954 now permit divorce and judicial separation. The right to divorce has been introduced in Hindu society not to attack the sacramental nature of marriage but to enable women to get rid of husbands who humiliate and torture them or who fail to fulfill their marital obligations.

Most times, custody of children is the biggest deadlock in divorce cases. The Law Commission in its report on "removal of discrimination against women in matters relating to the guardianship and custody of minor children and elaboration of the welfare principle" has recommended far-reaching changes. It has emphasized that there is no reason to accord a superior or preferential position to the father as opposed to the mother regarding custody of minor children. The Law Commission has also suggested the changed definition of a minor from a child less than five years of age to a child less than twelve years of age. It has further recommended that the custody of a minor child should normally be with the mother unless she has remarried and the father has not. In no circumstances should the child, specially a girl, be forced to live with a step father. In case both the parents have remarried, the court may entrust the child's custody to either of the grandparents, both paternal and maternal having equal rights.

Hindu Adoption and Maintenance Act, 1956 was the first law to legally recognize adoption. It permits the adoption of a son or a daughter with the consent of both husband and wife if they have no son or daughter of their own. An unmarried woman, a widow and a divorcee are also given the right to adopt a child. A married Hindu woman can adopt only if her husband renounced the world or has become insane or has changed his religion.

Abortion, i.e., the artificial termination of pregnancy, has been practised for long for health reasons, family planning or for personal reasons. Legally, however, abortion was treated as a criminal offence till 1970. In 1971 the Medical Termination of Pregnancy Act, 1971 was passed which legally permitted a pregnant woman as well as an abortionist to cause miscarriage. The Act, which came into force in April 1972, permits the termination of pregnancy by a registered doctor if the pregnancy does not exceed 12 weeks. But if the pregnancy exceeds 12 weeks, but not 20 weeks, not less than two doctors can terminate the pregnancy. The pregnancy is to be terminated if it involves risk to the life of the pregnant woman, grave injury to her physical and/or mental health and the risk that if the child is born, he/she would suffer from such physical or mental abnormalities so as to be seriously handicapped. The termination of pregnancy is also permitted where the pregnancy is caused by rape or failure of contraceptive device. The law of abortion is strict in two respects: firstly abortion can be performed only by a registered medical practioner, and secondly no termination of pregnancy is allowed at a place other than a hospital or a place approved by the government. If the pregnant woman is not minor (under 18 years of age), her prior consent for the termination of pregnancy is essential. In case a woman is a minor or a lunatic, the consent of her guardian is to be taken.

Women in India generally remained inactive and uninterested in the public and political life of the country till the second decade of the twentieth century. Political awareness and political participation of women varies with the levels of education, degree of urbanism in a given area, exposure to mass media, quality of local leadership, approach of political groups functioning in the area, and so forth. Two important political rights sanctioned to women by the Indian Constitution are female enfranchisement and eligibility for the legislature. As I have shown earlier, women's suffrage was achieved only in the 1920s in most parts even of the developed world. The demand for women' suffrage in India was first made in 1917 but the Southborrough Franchise Committee rejected it in 1918 arguing that women's suffrage would be out of harmony with the conservative feeling of the Indian women at this juncture when such large a proportion of male electors required education which is essential for a responsible vote. In 1919, on the recommendations of the joint selection committee, the Government of India Act, 1919 left the question of women's suffrage to the Indian provincial legislature. In 1932, the British government explicitly applied communal principles to women's franchise and representation. In the provincial legislature all seats including those reserved for women were allocated to members of specific communities and the electorates for each seat consisted of members of a single community. The Government of India Act, 1935 granted female enfranchisement on wifehood and education qualifications. Thus, about 9.0 per cent of the adult females were enfranchised in 1937. As a result, as many as 56 women entered the legislature in the 1937 elections. After independence, the number of women voters and women's representatives in parliament and assemblies has increased tremendously.

Women have suffered inferior position in Hindu and Mohammedean personal laws. According to Manu women should be held by their protectors in a status of subjection always. In Mohammedan law too women have received inferior treatment.[55] Christianity and Judaism hold women responsible for the First Sin and the consequent corrupted nature of humanity.

In feudal societies, power depended on status, customs and the then prevailing system of social organization. With the advent of Laissez-Faire economy and industrialization, the focus shifted to individual enterprise and capacity to compete on equal basis. The state took the role of an umpire at the best making the competition increasingly fair and equitable. A new era of social justice and social engineering through rule of law started with the emergency of the modern social welfare state and human rights jurisprudence. Law is being used as an instrument for distribution of rights and duties, resources and opportunities in such a way that equality of opportunities is so organized that the weak are duly protected and the minimum needs for enjoyment of life are made available to all.

With the advancement of society, women's liberation movement is getting momentum and no country can afford to ignore the position of women in national life. Law has been an instrument of economic and social change in all the democratic countries. In India, economic and social upliftment of women was initiated with the adoption of the Constitution in 1950. To make the spirit of the Constitution real and meaningful, the State resorted to a variety of social welfare laws empowering the weaker sections of society with preferential rights, benefits and entitlements. In determination of policies and priorities, in choice of strategies and approaches, in the distribution of resources and authority of the state, law became a critical input. Protection and welfare of women is an example of such use of the law.

In early societies, women as a class did not enjoy equal rights and opportunities as men had as the social attitudes and customs towards women got institutionalized through law and reinforced through political process. It is only from the beginning of the present century that the legal status of women came to be considered objectively in different legal systems. While there are differences in details, all legal systems display attributes of a male dominated society in theory and in practice. The Indian Constitution does not allow this disparity and discrimination. The Constitution of India guarantees all the rights to women which are given to men.

The constitution provides not only for the system of government but also sets the direction for the economic and social progress of the country. The Indian Constitution besides attempting to organize society through democratic processes, ensures the dignity of the human being and guarantees the finest values of liberty, equality and justice. The makers of the constitution very well realized that the law had to work as an instrument of social change. They, therefore, **guaranteed to every citizen certain basic rights and** commanded the state to follow certain social policies directed towards justice to every section of society which is explicit in the preamble, the fundamental rights and the directive principles of state policy. The constitution provides for equality before law and equal protection of the laws. Recognizing the traditional discriminatory practices against women and the need for preferential discrimination to fight them, the constitution has enabled the state to pass laws wherever necessary to give special rights and benefits to women.

The fundamentals of the Indian Constitution are contained in its Preamble which secures to its citizens Justice – social, economic and political; liberty of thought, expression, belief, faith and worship; equality of status and of opportunity; and to promote among them all fraternity assuring the dignity of the individual and the unity of and integrity of the nation. The theme of these objectives permeates throughout the entire constitution. It was to give effect to these objectives that fundamental rights and directive principles of state policy were enacted in Part III and Part IV of the Constitution and through them it was sought to achieve and maintain the dignity of individual.

The absolute concept of liberty and equality are very difficult to achieve in modern welfare society. That is why fundamental rights have been provided not in absolute terms. The form in which such rights have been provided is in the form of restrictions which the government is expected to follow in the governance of the country. However, the enjoyment of these rights is subject to the interest of the people. The state may, therefore, encroach on the domains of these rights for the common good or common interest. The question whether a fundamental right should be subjected to restrictions for the common good or public interest will depend on the conditions and circumstances prevailing at a particular time. The Constitution provides, firstly equal status to women in relation to men and secondly, preferential treatment in favour of women. In view of women's status of subservience, the preferential treatment in favour of women is not based on sex discrimination but on societal facts attached to women as a class.

The Constitution guarantees to every person the fundamental right not to be denied by the state, equality before the law or the equal protection of laws within the territory of India. (Article 14) It prohibits the state to discriminate against any citizen on ground only of religion, race, caste, sex, place of birth or any of them, (Article 15) ensures equality of opportunity for all citizens in matters related to employment or appointment to any office under the state (Article 16(1) and provides that no citizen shall, on grounds, inter alia, of sex be ineligible for, or discriminated against in respect of, any employment of office under the state. (Article 16(2) Article 16 is an instance of the application of the general rule of equality before law laid down in Article 14 and the prohibition of discrimination guaranteed by Article 15(1) with special reference to the opportunity for employment or appointment to any office under the state.

Apart from the guarantee of equality, the constitution provides for special protection and preferential treatment in favour of women. Clause (3) of Article 15 says that "nothing in this Article (Article 15) shall prevent the State from making any special provision for women and children. The clause embodies exception to the prohibition contained in clauses (1) and (2) of Article 15. From reading clauses (1) and (2) together it follows that while there can be no discrimination in general on the ground of sex, special provision in the case of women and children are permissible. Thus, it would be no violation of Article 15 if institutions are set up by the state exclusively for women and places reserved for women at public entertainments or in public conveyances. The special position given to women in regard to the offence of adultery (The Indian Penal Code, Section 497) was held valid under this clause. Section 354 of the Indian Penal Code is not invalid because it protects the modesty only of women and section 488 (now 125) of the criminal code is valid although it obliges the husband to maintain his wife but not vice versa.

The language of clause (3) Article 15 is in absolute terms and does not appear to be restricted in any way the nature or ambit of special provisions which the State may make in favour of women. The Supreme Court has held that the special provision referred to in clause (3) need not be restricted to measures which are beneficial in the strict sense. The decision of excise authorities to prefer men over women in granting licenses for opening liquor shops was struck down as coming within the prohibition of Article 15 (1) and not saved by Article 15 (3).

Besides fundamental rights, the Directive Principles of State Policy contained in Part IV of the Constitution directs the State to take certain measures for the protection of the welfare of women. According to these principles, the State is required to strive to promote the welfare of the people by securing and protecting as effectively as it may, a social order in which justice – social, economic and political – shall inform all the institutions of the national life, to direct its policy in particular towards securing that the citizens, men and women equally, have the right to an adequate means of livelihood, that there is equal pay for equal work for both men and women, that the health and strength of workers, men and women, and the tender age of children are not abused and that citizens are not forced by economic necessity to enter a vocation unsuited to their age or strength and to make provision for securing just and human conditions of work and for maternity relief. (Articles 49 and 42)

The Directive Principles of State Policy set out the aims and objectives to be taken up by the state in the governance of the country. These principles are the expressions of the socio-economic objectives of the Constitution. The idea of welfare state envisaged by our Constitution can only be achieved if the State endeavoured to implement them with a high sense of moral duty. It indicates that the framers of the Constitution wanted to establish economic democracy. These principles constitute a very comprehensive political, social and economic programme for a modern democratic state. The Directive Principles of State Policy differ in one vital respect from the fundamental rights incorporated in the Constitution. Whereas the former are unenforceable rights, the latter are enforceable rights. They still form part of constitutional laws of the land. Directive Principles of State Policy and Fundamental Rights together constitute the 'conscience' of the Constitution, and represent the basic rights inherent in human beings in this country. Both are in fact equally fundamental and efforts should be made to harmonize them by imparting the Directive Principles in the Construction of Fundamental Rights.

Besides the special provisions discussed above, Article 23 of the Constitution forbids 'traffic in human beings'. This Article embodies two declarations. First, that traffic in human beings, beggars and other similar forms of forced labour, are prohibited. The prohibition applies not only to state but also to private persons, bodies and organizations. Second, any contravention of the prohibition shall be an offence punishable in accordance with law. Under Article 35 of the Constitution, laws punishing acts prohibited by these Articles shall only be made by parliament, though existing laws on the subject, until altered or repealed by parliament are saved. Traffic in human beings means to deal in men and women like goods, such as to sell or let or otherwise dispose them of. Though there is no clear provision in the Article directly forbidding traffic in women – the most prevalent of this sort of exploitation – the expression 'traffic in human beings' would include traffic in women for immoral or other purposes. The suppression of Immoral Traffic (Prevention Act, 1956) is a law made by Parliament under Article 35 of the Constitution for the purpose of punishing acts which result in traffic in human beings.

It is one of the fundamental duties of every citizen of India to renounce practices derogatory to the dignity of women. (Article 51-A [e]) The fundamental duty which is added by the 42nd Amendment of the Constitution in 1976, in addition to creating and promoting a culture, also strengthens the hands of the legislature in enforcing these duties vis-à-vis the fundamental rights. Since the duties are imposed upon the citizens and not upon the state, legislation is necessary for their implementation.

The above analysis of the women's rights shows that women in India have a satisfactory degree of rights. But the question is whether women in India are aware of their rights. As I have shown earlier in this chapter, a right claimed by one individual or section of individuals enforces certain duties on another individual, section of individuals or State. Hence, constitutional and legal provision of women's rights do not necessarily grant these rights to them concretely, unless women are aware of them, consciously claim them, fight for them and men, especially, and women in the society act in accordance with the obligation placed on them by these rights. Awareness of women's rights needs to be cultivated also among men so that they act in duty towards the granting of these rights. Further, mechanisms to increase the ability of women to exercise their rights need to be promoted by governments and society in general. A societal conviction on the rights of women is the panacea for women's empowerment.

Proper implementation and application of laws in practice is lacking in our country. Therefore, we do not have satisfactory results in the sphere of women's rights. Many are the reasons for this state of affairs: non-availability of easy access to justice including the lack of information or knowledge about them by the victims (women's legal illiteracy), reluctance of women to have recourse to legal process in Indian social situation and expensive legal process. To facilitate emancipation of women, legal literacy must be emphasized as an important aspect of women's education. Free and competent legal aid should be available to women to choose legal process. There should be structural and procedural changes in the system of administration of justice which includes establishment of special institutions like family courts, employment of more women personnel in the legal system, immediate and positive action in reported cases of the violation of women's rights, particularly cases of atrocities against women etc. Voluntary and non-governmental social action groups and organizations should be encouraged to come forward to facilitate access to justice, administration of justice and implementation of justice. Now there is need to inculcate the constitutional values and legal norms into the society and create a feeling of fraternity towards women in the people having power and authority in the society and also among the masses.

The state is constitutionally permitted to discriminate in favour of women, if such discrimination is found necessary. Women constitute the largest minority in India with a variety of social and economic disabilities which prevent them from exercising their legal and conventional rights. Selecting one's mate is disapproved, widow marriage is socially prohibited, divorce is looked down upon and inheritance of paternal property is denied under different pretexts. Hundreds of cases of ill treatment of girls by their in-laws or their husbands for failure to bring adequate dowry are reported in newspapers regularly. The number of suicides and wife burning are also increasing by the day. So discriminatory protection may still be necessary for the vast majority of Indian women. But such policies are to be avoided as far as possible. The 218th paragraph of the document of 4th World Conference on Women at Beijing in 1995 says:

> In order to protect the human rights of women, it is necessary to avoid, as far as possible, resorting to reservations and to ensure that no reservation is incompatible with the object and purpose of the Convention or is otherwise incompatible with international treaty law. Unless the human rights of women, as defined by international human rights instruments, are fully recognized and effectively protected, applied, implemented and enforced in national law as well as in national practice in family, civil, penal, labour and commercial codes and administrative rules and regulations, they will exist in name only.

However, laws are not the only discriminatory aspects that are to be changed. Women's situation has to undergo a transformation. No doubt, the Constitution of India has given the right to women to contest for legislature and executive bodies, say, from the Panchayat to the parliament. Yet, in reality, women are denied these rights. The key positions in the polity are not for them. A woman's progress is confined to flamboyant declarations and speeches. Capable and talented women are unjustly ignored on the ground of sex. This is the general condition. Two or three women in high offices do not alter the situation. Naturally all socially conscious women are intensely thinking over the issue of overcoming male chauvinism on the one hand, and transcending the barrier placed by the present social system on the other.

Women's liberation does not mean hatred of men. How can one half of humanity hate another half? How can a woman hate her husband, father sons, brothers and cousins? At the same time, she does not like to be trampled upon and treated like a beast of burden. She is a human being with inherent dignity and self-respect on which she can never compromise or surrender. Women do not desire greater privileges or higher status than men. What they demand is equality. Except the additional capacity to give birth to children, the women's talents and capabilities are on par with those of men. Of course, her service to humanity in perpetuating the human race has to be respected and honoured. Women's emancipation has to be total, in all sectors of life – social, cultural, political and economic. Women cannot be socially and culturally free but kept politically and economically a slave or dependent because the latter situation will endanger the former.

REFERENCES

1. John Locke, *Second Treatise on Civil Government*, Paragraph 4 in Frederick A. Olafson, ed., *Society, Law, and Morality : Readings in Social Philosophy from Classical and Contemporary Sources* (New Jersey: Prentice-Hall, 1961) p.118
2. *Ibid.*, Paragraph 6, p.119

3. *Ibid.*, Paragraph 88, p.131
4. *Ibid.*, Paragraphs 124, 134 & 138, pp.137, 139 & 141
5. Thomas Hobbes, *Leviathan*, Chapter XIII, in Frederick A. Olafson, ed., *Society, Law, and Morality : Readings in Social Philosophy from Classical and Contemporary Sources* (New Jersey: Prentice-Hall, 1961) p.79
6. *Ibid.*, Chapter XIV; p.81
7. Jean-Jacques Rousseau, *A Discourse on the Origin of Inequality*, in Frederick A. Olafson, ed., *Society, Law, and Morality : Readings in Social Philosophy from Classical and Contemporary Sources* (New Jersey: Prentice-Hall, 1961) pp.195-96
8. *Ibid.*, Book IX; p.205
9. Immanuel Kant, *The Science of Right*, Introduction in Frederick A. Olafson, ed., *Society, Law, and Morality : Readings in Social Philosophy from Classical and Contemporary Sources* (New Jersey: Prentice-Hall, 1961) p.151
10. *Ibid.*, p.152
11. Ralph Mason Blake, "On Natural Rights," Readings in Ethical Theory, Wilfrid Sellars and John Hospers, eds., Second Edition (New Jersey: Prentice-Hall, 1970) pp. 567-68, 571
12. *Universal Declaration of Human Rights of the United Nations* as adopted in 10 December 1948, Article 1
13. *Ibid.*, Preamble
14. H. J. McCloskey, "Respect for Human Moral Rights versus Maximizing Good," *Utility and Rights*, R. G. Frey, ed. (Oxford: Basil Blackwell, 1985) pp.125-26
15. H. J. McCloskey, "Respect for Human Moral Rights versus Maximizing Good," Utility and Rights, R. G. Frey, ed. (Oxford: Basil Blackwell, 1985) p.126
16. *The UN World Conference on Women* at Beijing; "Platform for Action", paragraph 213
17. Please see Andrew Byrnes, "Women, Feminism and International Human Rights Law - Methodological Myopia, Fundamental Flaws or Meaningful Marginalisation?: Some Current Issues," in www.hrw.org quoted from *12th Australian Year Book of International Law*, pp.205-240

18. Barbara R. Cruikshank "Patriarchy," *Microsoft® Encarta® 98 Digital Encyclopedia.* © 1993-1997 Microsoft
19. *Ibid.*
20. D. Dale Cosper, "Simone de Beauvoir," *Microsoft® Encarta® 98 Digital Encyclopedia.* © 1993-1997 Microsoft Corporation.
21. Simone de Beauvoir, *The Second Sex* (1949) as quoted in D. Dale Cosper, "Simone de Beauvoir"
22. Barbara R. Cruikshank, "Patriarchy"
23. *Document of the Fourth UN World Conference on Women*, Paragraphs 216, 220, 223, 224 and 225
24. *The Bhagavad Gita*, V:18; paraphrase
25. Kautalya, *Arthasastra* : 1.19.33
26. Ap. Dh. S., 11
27. *Manusmriti*, XI, 176-77, 188
28. *Ibid.*, VIII, 416
29. *Ibid.*, IX, 195
30. *Ibid.*, IX, 196
31. *Ibid.*, IX, 197
32. *Rgveda* X. 85.13.38
33. *Kautalya*, 111.2
34. *Manusmriti*, IX.194
35. *On Yajnavalkya*, 11.143
36. *Dayabhaga,* IV.I.182-83
37. Henry Maine, *The Early History of Institution*, p.231
38. *Manusmriti*, IX, 199
39. *Kautilya*, III, 2.152
40. *Yajnavalkya*, II, 150
41. *On Yajnavalkya* II.147
42. *Kautilya*, III.2.153
43. *Manusmriti*, IV, 192-93
44. *Ibid.*, IV, 195
45. *Ibid.*, IV, 197
46. *Yajnavalkya*, II, 117, 144
47. *Ap. Kn. S.* II.6.14.2.3

48. *Kautilya*, III. 5
49. *Gautama*, XXVIII.21
50. *Manusmriti*, IX, 185-86, 189
51. *Vishnu*, XVII, 43
52. *Manusmriti*, IX.187
53. *Narad*, XIII.52
54. *On Yajnavalkya*, II.136
55. Anirudh Prasad, *Social Engineering and Constitutional Protection of Weaker Sections in India* (New Delhi: Deep and Deep Publications, 1980) p.87

5

Violation of the Rights of Women

The evolution of every human being – man or woman – starts right from the time a single cell divides and multiplies building up trillions of cells around itself to create an organism endowed with consciousness. Like a man, a woman begins her journey of life at birth and passes through different stages till her lifespan is over. In this journey, she develops different characteristics, undergoes physical and psychological changes, acquires maturity and with the advancement of time contributes her share in the progress of the society. Unlike man, however, for most of the time she remains latent in many spheres, activities and decisions and does not get the credit she deserves. No wonder, history has recorded the names and achievements of a large number of men but of only a very small number of women.

The attitude of the ancient societies towards women was conditioned by her various relationships with man. The ancient Indian society was no exception. As a wife, a mother, a sister and a daughter, she was respected and loved. For her fundamental qualities of nourishing, conserving and inspiring, she was praised. She was an asset like the *Brahmanas*, children and cows were, and as such she received all protection, care and enjoyed various types of privileges.

At the same time, named as a weak creature, she was subjected to certain controls, restrictions and prohibitions. Woman as a member of the opposite sex was an object of infatuation and admiration to a successful lover while she was the cause of wild complaints by a rejected and disappointed one. As an object of distraction, she was to be avoided and to an ascetic and a man of retiring temperament as well as to kings and heroes she was an obstacle and an object of condemnation. The epics, comprehensive as they are in their scope and treatment, depict woman in all these aspects.

The factors that enhanced women's prestige were motherhood and their inspiring and nourishing roles. It was difficult for primitive man to understand the concept of 'paternity'. Therefore, it was natural for him to respect the mysterious power of fertility possessed by women, which inspired in him awe and respect for her. This power, together with the great self-sacrificing qualities of motherhood, was the woman's greatest asset. It led to mother worship in all primitive and ancient civilizations from the Mediterranean to the Indus valley. In countries like Egypt and Babylon this respect was also reflected in their laws. In ancient India mother worship took deep roots. Woman not only plays her great part in man's creation but by her vital charm she inspires and energizes him. Indians thus believed women's nature to be the human manifestation of the universal *Sakti* (power), which is also her charm.

Another quality in woman, for which she has been greatly prized by man, was her power of conserving and nourishing life. Man is able to earn but in his outdoor struggle he is not able to store up his wealth for the future and the family. These functions are admirably performed by woman. She has been, therefore, considered as goddess of prosperity in Indian literature including the Epics.

For all these qualities as a mother and wife, woman has been accorded respect in the Epics. However, respect, kind treatment and even material gifts that she received had ulterior motives. In other words, she was respected because on her depended the righteousness of men, all the enjoyments and pleasures, the begetting and nourishing of offspring and the accomplishments of all the acts which are indispensable for society. A person desiring affluence and prosperity was required to honour them, for the presence of women so honoured was as propitious as that of the goddess of prosperity. As a warning, it is stated that if in some families due to the bad treatment they receive, women indulge in sorrow, no effort or deed would bear fruit and such families would soon become extinct. No greater homage can be paid to women than to say that they are the light of the home, mother of the universe and the supporters of the earth with all its forests.

The honour and respect accorded to women was also reflected in manners prescribed in the Epics. The right to pass was to be conceded to a woman and to a disabled person even prior to a man with heavy load or to a king. In the didactic portions of the epics, which however indicate deterioration in the status of women, a *brahmana*, a cow, a king and an old man are given precedence over her in this matter. This attitude was, however, due to the fact that all of them were accorded great reverence in society and the *Brahmanas* had precedence even over the queens. May be these were later customs interpolated in the Epic stories. Respect to elderly ladies was shown not only by touching their feet but by walking round them while taking leave.

There is another side of the coin too. It was natural for primitive man to feel important for giving support and protection to women during the crucial time of her life (i.e., during child birth). Had it not been for this support, the human race would have been exterminated. According to sociologists and feminists, this dependence led to degradation of the status of women. Although physical weakness is one of the reasons of degradation of woman and was responsible for her many disabilities, it is hard to estimate its effect. In the Epics as an *abala* she has been assigned a degraded position. But her weakness also inspired a sense of chivalry in heroes, and so as far as one can make out, '*bhiru*' in the Epics, is a term more of endearment than of contempt.

The idea of chivalry led to compassion being shown towards the weak, and therefore, also to women. Sugriva sends Tara to pacify angry Lakshmana, for he thinks that great men do not ill treat women. He is right in his judgement as later events prove. For the same reason, Hanuman shows mercy upon the *Rakshasi* Lanka. A hero was expected to keep cool and smiling before women. Cruel behaviour towards women has been condemned in an oath-taking. A hater of women was considered to be a very low fellow. It is, however, said that untruth was permissive where women were concerned but still this was not considered an ideal behaviour.

Nevertheless, the narrative part of the Epics depicts some rough manners and easy morals which seem revolting to the modern mind. The dread of the ladies when a conqueror entered a conquered city does not speak much of the sense of chivalry. There can be no parallel to the pawning of Draupadi, a great blot on Yudhisthira who committed the initial mistake. It must, however, be borne in mind that this custom was a survival of the past and is indicative of the wife's position as the property of the husband. According to the Vedic tradition, a wife lost at stakes was degraded to the position of a *dâsi*. But the insults and the inhuman treatment meted out to Draupadi in the assembly are revolting to any cultured mind. It goaded the Pandavas to war and a terrible revenge. This crude behaviour not objected to and thus quietly supported by the Kauravas, even their learned old men, was exaggerated in order to paint perfect villains or rough warriors of old, who in their jealousy forgot the finer and nobler sentiments. Nevertheless, the frequent references to the event with regret and condemnation indicate that such a behaviour was not approved even by the wives of the Kauravas, not to say of the greater section of the civil society, for it was due to the representation of the arch villain's mother, i.e., Gandhari, that Draupadi was granted freedom. Therefore, these exceptions prove that the society on the whole was for showing respect and compassion to women. The ideal, which was followed by Yudhishthira, the son of Dharma, was different. When the Kuru ladies were abducted by the Gandharva, he forced his brother to rescue them.

For the disparaging attitude towards women, other biological reasons must also therefore be looked for. There has been a feeling of contamination and impurity for every waste product of the human body. This, it seems, led to the belief that woman was contaminated, impure and was to be avoided during menstrual period and child birth. It thus resulted in the seclusion of women during puberty all over the world and periodical segregation of women thereafter.

In ancient Indian literature as well as in the Epics, it is narrated that Indra incurred the sin of the murder of a Brahmana and he slid the Brahmana into four parts. One of these parts was taken by a woman. This explains her excommunication from society like a Brahmahan, i.e., murderer of a Brahmana, during the menstrual period. This was one of the reasons for the loss of her religious status and rights.

Despite these taboos, woman as an object of pleasure was desired by all men. But the primitive man was not able to understand the psycho-physical tiredness due to intemperance. The distraction and loss of energy which he felt due to it, was naturally associated with the malefic influence of woman, who was considered an agent of weakness. Therefore, when strength was needed, i.e., during hunting and fishing expeditions, contact with woman was tabooed. The same reason may be forwarded for the advice given to warriors and kings to avoid her lest they may feel effeminate and weak as a result of excessive indulgence. There is little difference between savage and warrior-like ideas of gaining physical strength by avoiding contact with woman and ascetic ideas of conserving psychic or mental strength through continence. Therefore, whenever man indulged in adventurous, ambitious or world-forsaking pursuits, woman as a source of distraction, alluring and arresting him in home and hearth, has been painted as the cause of his degradation and was to be avoided.

The ascetic ideal emphasized the transience of the world and preached the renunciation of all objects of desire. Naturally, it led to propaganda against woman, who was the greatest object of desire and the central figure of family life. To the composers of the Great Epic, Buddhism and Jainism were known. Even before the advent of these sects, ascetics were carrying on their propaganda against the woman and her vile character. Thus many parts of the *Mahabharata*, thought to be of a later origin, which depict the ascetic attitude to life, are full of condemnation of women. Nothing can be asserted about the knowledge of Buddhism on the part of the composer of the *Ramayana*. The ascetic way of life has not been so much stressed in the *Ramayana* as in the didactic portions of the Great Epic.

Jaratkaru's story clearly indicates how the position of the wife deteriorated due to ascetic ideals. Sage Jaratkaru did not marry on account of such ideals but later when he got a progeny, he did not perform the duty of a husband. When his motive was served, he left his wife without any fault on her part. This shows how little regard he had for her. This instance also indicates that the importance of sons might have persuaded even ascetics to take wives. Perhaps in order to avoid such occurrences, it was stated later that through penance sons could be born. It was even propounded that great *Rshis* had sons through miracles.

Women appear as objects of pity for they were given gifts and food in charity along with the old and the invalid, although according to one passage gifts given to women were one of the sixteen useless gifts.

It will suffice to say that impurity imposed upon the woman, lack of education, admission of non-Aryan women into Aryan families, may all have been responsible for her exclusion from the Vedic sacrificial religion. She took to the new *Puranika* religion and satisfied her religious urge. The harm done to the woman by such excommunication was that she now began to be classed among the *Sudras*. Her intellectual growth was retarded as she was denied the only intellectual education in the Veda and *Sankhya* philosophy of that time. Women and the *Sudras* were allowed to practice yoga and they were regarded as being capable of attaining emancipation. Women in general offered prayers to female divinities, trees, goddesses, rivers and invoked fate which is indicative of their helplessness as well as of their superstitious nature. Loss of intellectual activity and religious status may have been responsible for the loss of their rights as well.

The birth of a female child evokes many responses from the family ranging from an overall sense of indifferent acceptance to a sense of contentment and a feeling of being blessed. It is in this context that a girl develops an emotive map of the family. The parent's indifferent acceptance of her makes the female child realize that her status and her rights are secondary and she experiences no space for herself. She learns to accept herself as an unwanted or as a transient object to be cared for, but never to belong. In the process, she starts doubting her value as a person. Indian social system emphasizes such qualities as obedience, self-sacrifice, responsibility and expects women to prove an asset to both her parent's and husband's families. Women thus derive security from the fact that they are being perceived as being desirable in appearance, in conduct and in being useful around the home. Each of these modes of security is then linked to their future. Being desirable in appearance ensures a girl a good husband. Desirability in personal and social conduct is associated with adjustment and acceptance by the in-laws and with being successful in her roles as wife and mother. These roles stress that she has to be tolerant, patient, nurturing, fostering, calm, quiet – a resilient force which is not visible but always present. Women's part is supposed to be in the conserving and propagation of race, and these functions are thought to be naturally inherited by them. However, in the process of moulding herself to come up to the expectations of her social role, a woman generally finds no clear-cut anchors for her own psychological location either within herself or in the system. Thus, girls in Indian setup more often than not lack the sense of self-respect and do not learn to value themselves. In spite of having all capabilities and potentialities present in them, they are generally ignorant about their worth. In this manner their own self images get deformed irrevocably over years. An Indian woman generally perceives herself in terms of various dos and don'ts of the social order as is depicted in the following Marathi street verse "A girl is Born."

Do not abandon the vow of womanhood taken by you:
You have to mind the hearth and children,
Do not ask odd questions, do not exceed the boundaries,
Do not get out of control.
Do not abandon the vow of womanhood:
Do not speak with your face up, be inside the house,
Wash clothes, clean utensils, cook and serve food,
Observe the fasts and perform *Vratas*,
Bend your neck downwards, look downwards,

Walk without looking up, do not let your eyes wander.

This image of femininity is developed in the woman before she is old enough to realize that there are two sexes. Right from her childhood days, a considerable importance is attached to the way a girl carries herself, the way she sits, stands, talks and interacts with others. A girl has to be careful about her posture; she should not sit cross-legged. She is encouraged to speak softly and avoid abrasive male language. Shyness and modesty are approved and considered natural feminine qualities. A female infant is often dressed in so called feminine colours such as pink, red etc. A male infant may be dressed in brown, grey etc. Parents reinforce dependency in girls and achievements and assertiveness in boys. By providing appropriate toys, dresses and by encouraging sex appropriate play activities, parents instill sex role stereotypes at an early age. Among boys such traits as 'real boy', 'leader', 'good at games' and 'takes chance' make for popularity. Among girls, traits like 'quiet', 'not a show off,' 'not quarrelsome,' 'doll like' are rated more closely to popularity rating.[1]

It is within these stereotypical limits that women question their situation, express resentment, use manipulative strategies – often against other women –, turn deprivation and self denial into sources of power and attempt to carve out a living space for themselves. There exists remarkable sex differences in self-concept and role-concept but the sex differences in the psychological domain are insignificant and inconsistent as shown by the findings of Maccoby and Jackline[2] and Pleck.

Starting with differences in intellectual capacity, there is no substantial evidence of an overall difference in the capacities of men and women.[3] The difference, however, is in certain special abilities. To illustrate, on the basis of researches, it can be said that girls are more fluent verbally, can memorize well, tend to be passive and are superior in perceptual speed and manual dexterity.[4] With regard to mathematical reasoning, male superiority is the rule; it does not hold good for simple calculations or when mathematical problems are given in verbal forms. Girls are reported to be somewhat inferior in mechanical aptitude but women are superior in their aptitude for clerical work of all sorts. Benett[5] reported that very little difference between the sexes on both verbal and numerical aptitude scores actually existed. Maccoby and Jackline reported that males and females are alike in more respects than is commonly supposed. Therefore, male superiority is not in any way due to inferiority of women but it develops as a part of their educational process.

It is found that girls do not place enough emphasis on professional or occupational success as boys do.[6] Left to their own devices, a large proportion of boys are likely to make vocational choices in the professional areas, whether or not their level of intelligence and academic success warrants such a choice. On the other hand, girls are not motivated to aspire to the positions their abilities would make it possible. Walter and Marzolf[7] showed that girls of all grade levels marked significantly lower goal discrepancy scores, i.e., they set their sights lower or nearer to their actual performance. This lesser degree of ambition which is characteristic of younger and older girls is called 'low' achievement motive. It is found that women lack the need to achieve in three related areas – education, employment and income. This tendency on the part of women is attributed by Western psychologists to 'fear to succeed'. According to Martina Hornes,[8] who pioneered this direction of research in the U.S., women unlike men, deliberately limit their achievement in competitive situations. Their reasons for doing so presumably included fear of loss of femininity, social isolation and rejection by others. It is also because they are basically anxious, insecure, dependent and more concerned about social repute.[9] Further it is argued that females are not motivated to achieve per se and that their success in society is largely a function of their need for affiliation. It can, therefore, be pointed out that low achievement behaviour of women is an outcome of a unique and inherent personality disposition owing to their sex role orientation with no reference to their subordinate status in the society. Thus the inference is that women avoid success because of sex role training. Since achievement demands aggressiveness, which in majority of research reports is more among males than is in females,[10] women naturally tend to shy away because of their basic nurturing disposition.

Feminist scholars have also argued the fact that women's low achievement success is not due to any inherent personality trait. Rather, it is the material resultant of the prevailing social structure. Blueman[11] and Sheila Rothman[12] for instance, have attempted to explain women's subordinate status in the occupational sphere in terms of sexual segregation. The crux of their argument is that males occupy a predominant position because of their total control of all resources in the society. Going a step ahead, Jean Miller[13] has shown how this kind of subordination affects women's personalities. Miller observes that it is the past conditioning and fear of punishment from the powerful that make women subordinate, avoid autonomy and success, rather than any inherent personality disposition.

In contrast to this situation with regard to adult achievement, numerous studies on school achievement confirm that girls consistently make better school grades than boys usually till their late teens. It has also been observed that girls are less frequently retarded and are more frequently accelerated than boys. Many of them even receive higher marks than boys.[14] Analysis of the results of matriculation examination[15] has shown that school achievement is significantly higher and in favour of girls. But why girls do not continue to show the same trend after the school days are over? Probably, the most plausible explanation for sex differences in school achievement can be offered by relating these to the differences in attitudes and personality traits like docility and submissiveness (usually considered feminine traits which are themselves a function of socio-cultural factors). These traits may enable girls to make a better impression on teachers than boys do. At the same time, these traits may, to some extent, prevent them from assuming positions of leadership in the world of affairs. This can also be because girls perceive themselves as somewhat lacking in basic qualities necessary for success such as assertiveness, independence and competence and also capability for doing well academically and in tasks, being less confident about their future performance.

The discussion about psychological characteristics will remain incomplete without making a mention of the status of females' non-intellectual interests and values. The distinctly feminine interests are indicated on items having to do with (i) musical, artistic activities, (ii) literary activities, (iii) certain kinds of people, (iv) certain forms of entertainment, e.g., fortune telling, full dress functions and movies dealing with social problems, (v) clerical work, (vi) teaching, (vii) social work, (viii) window shopping, and (ix) certain school subjects.[16] It is generally seen that girls are more interested in aesthetic, social and clerical jobs.

Hence, women's psyche, values and interests seem to be in line with the sex stereotypes prevailing in society. These typical feminine interests represent the general attitude and outlook of a woman who does not want a career for its own sake, but who is satisfied to pursue any pleasant congenial activity until marriage and even afterwards. In the study of values as observed by Allport and his group of researchers,[17] women obtain higher average scores for aesthetic, social and religious values indicating more concern for the welfare of others as goals for living. Men obtained higher average scores for theoretical, economic and political success and showed more desire for influence and power over others as goals for living.

In contrast to the difference in interests which appear at a very tender age, other personality differences appear between boys and girls at their high school age.[18] In one of the studies, it has been reported that women are more neurotic, less self-sufficient, more introvert, less dominant and more socially dependent than men. Findings show that there is a tendency for women's average to be closer to the maladjusted end of the scale than men's.[19]

From the above discussion, two facts emerge. First, there are few differences between males and females during early years of life. Second, women's personality, ability, behavioural adjustments are inferior to that of men as age increases. Not only this – certain negative tendencies are noticed among women in general. These conclusions have serious implications for the personality integration of women, their self-actualization, output and productivity from the point of view of modern humanistic psychologists like Maslow[20] and Erickson.[21]

Why do women lag behind men in several aspects of personality development as age increases? This is, first of all, not in any way connected to any intrinsic lack in women in comparison to men. The answer to the question posed may be found in what is now called cultural conditioning. Women's role in society is a social construct and they were neither allowed nor inclined to break free of this paradigm in which society expected them to be seen. Certain male perceptions connected women's supposed physical weakness with a certain fragility and tentativeness in their nature. This construction gave rise to the picture of women as feeble, needful of support, fickle, untrustworthy and tender. Any woman who wanted to be better than other women, the outstanding ones, also tried to improve on this given paradigm only so that society would then recognize her as 'good' or 'advanced' or 'educated' woman. If she wanted to break free of this paradigm, she was then not considered with respect or admiration. She was considered more a rebel than a woman of substance. Hence, most women tried to stick to the labels given and got worse in the company of other women in a typical joint-family setup, which promoted further deterioration of women's personality.

According to Carl Rogers, another humanistic psychologist, every organism continually strives to develop and expand itself and its motivation is focused on striving to achieve self-actualization. In and through the process of interpersonal and social experiences in the environment, an individual views himself/herself as a person and evaluates his/her worth at all times which leads to his/her further development. In order to achieve self-actualization, four conditions are necessary: (i) the person must be respected and loved by others; (ii) the person must respect and have faith in herself and her abilities to achieve her goal; (iii) the choice available to the individual must be clearly perceived because if the person is unaware of the choices, self-growth is hindered; and (iv) the choices must be clearly symbolized. The person must not only be aware of the alternative but he must also have clear cut descriptions and full understanding of choices.

Since the Indian woman commands little respect and love by society in general, she develops little respect and faith in herself and in her abilities to achieve her rights. Further, her self-growth is seriously hindered since the choices available to her are neither clearly defined and concretized nor presented clearly to enable her to internalize them over a period of time. Consequently, she more often than not, develops a deformed, inadequate, diffused and fragile self-image which exerts a stifling influence on her in the sphere of self-growth, vocational and social growth. No wonder, women are likely to remain helpless, dependent, docile and submissive individuals with weak ego strengths and ego integration. This state of affairs is itself a negative reinforcer to any worthwhile accomplishment and benumbs decision making, organizational ability and ability of self propulsion. These prove as strong barriers for individuals in self-actualization, progress, satisfaction and enjoying rights.

The above view is also supported by Erickson.[22] I believe that in case of Indian woman, the most crucial period in the development of self-identity is adolescence, the stage which Erickson considers important for role differentiation and emergence of identity. At this stage, a person seeks answers to the question 'who am I.' An Indian girl by dint of her barriers generally fails to answer this question which results in role diffusion and uncertainty in her identity. As a result of this, she seldom attains her full potential being mostly unaware of her assets and limitations. Abraham Cowley's words hold good for the frustration of women in Indian society: "Just as a bird that flies about/ And beats itself against the cage,/ Finding at last no passage out/ It sits and sings, and so overcomes its rage."

As a result of her multifarious but negative experiences, which a girl during infancy, childhood (early childhood, play age and school age), young adulthood, mature adulthood and old age in the Indian social setup undergoes, she develops distrust rather than hope, shame and doubt instead of autonomy and will, guilt instead of initiative, inferiority in place of competence, role confusion instead of solidarity of conviction, isolation rather than affiliation, stagnation instead of growth and despair in place of wisdom. Women, under these circumstances, can face traumatic situations and resolve their conflicts and anxieties in a productive and happy manner. Atrocities committed on women, female suicides and sufferings of women are direct corollaries of these circumstances. Thus, it can be said that women in the Indian social setup can be described as the victims of their own 'diseased psyches' which causes them to perceive themselves as helpless, incompetent and helpless creatures who cannot fight to acquire their own rights and looked down upon by significant others in their lives. Women themselves are responsible for the violation of their own rights, but one should not forget that any mind structured in a particular way cannot easily overcome the structured model. Much less, a full half of society, structured in a particular mould through power mechanisms and institutions like family, religion, politics and every other aspect of social life.

Women can be regarded as slaves to society and tradition. They are slaves to male domination. They are slaves to ignorance. Not only that, in social, economic, political and cultural sectors of life, they do not have freedom. They are slaves to their husbands and families. Women have no individuality. They are not allowed to aspire for individual freedom. A slave is purchased with money. But a woman goes into slavery paying the husband in the shape of dowry. The woman does not possess any right over her body. She has to beget children at the behest of her benign husband. Even if she wants to go in for permanent birth control operation, her husband's consent is sought. Although this is not required legally, powerful social conditioning makes a farce of the laws of the land. She is treated as an object of sex. Her lot is to remain silent even when she is abused, beaten and violated. She shall neither demur nor protest. She shall not complain even when her life is threatened. The society abhors a woman who goes to court to protect herself.

A working woman has to labour hard both in the office and at home. The husband cannot be expected to help her to any extent. An employed woman has no rights over her earning. She has to tender her wages or salary to her husband or at best, she has to spend it as per his directions. The law may speak differently, but tradition, custom and social practice dictate daily lives. She has the right of rearing children. But she has no rights over them. They are called his sons and his daughters. She cannot be the guardian of the children so long as her husband is alive. The case of a Muslim woman is much worse. She cannot act as the guardian unless she is appointed by a court of law. From the very time of birth, a woman is discriminated against. She is to be under the protection of a male as per the *Dharma Shastras*. The society is such that it will remain indifferent, nay, it does not condemn the husband even if he abuses her, beats her and burns her to death.

A woman has to be educated, beautiful and submissive. This is the view of a modern husband. This idea has been accepted even by educated women for generations, and is being acted upon by them. Thus, women steeped in ignorance, are enjoying their rights as slaves to the males and to the family. The woman is required to maintain the dignity and prestige of the family. She has to undertake responsibilities befitting a wife but she must not demand any rights of her own. If inequality is so grotesque, is it not a sign of slavery?

The woman is the first slave to the society bedeviled with tradition and orthodoxy. Like the slaves in the olden times, women do not know that they have a right to freedom and that they can aspire for freedom. They dedicate their lives to superstition, blind faith, traditional ideas and customs. Modernity, scientific outlook, rationalistic views, philosophical thoughts etc., are conspicuous by their absence among women. At every moment, for every event she shudders at the thought of society. The reason is pure and simple. Her belief in her inferiority to man is the root cause. That is exactly why she wishes to marry a man more educated than herself. She has no right to select her life-partner. If she is barren, the society blames her. The society abhors a divorcee. Even if a child widow marries, she is treated with contempt. A man is allowed to marry any number of times even if he is aged and has grown up children.

Woman is a slave to double morality in respect of sex. She shall be a virgin before marriage. After marriage she shall not have any sexual relations with any man except her husband. The man is under no such disabilities. A Muslim male can have four wives at one and the same time. Concubinage is winked at by society though it may afford a ground for divorce. A woman shall not be friends with a man outside the family. She has to wear *Ghungat* (veil) or observe *purdah*. Society treats her as unholy during the period of menses and confinement. In a case of debauchery, woman is abused. She is described as a fallen woman. The man goes scot-free. What is pleaded here is that there should be only one set of moral principles for both men and women. The view that education and employment are not necessary for women still prevails. Women cannot officiate as priests in temples, mosques and churches. They cannot recite 'mantras' in sacrificial ceremonies. They cannot conduct marriages.

The widow has to observe very hard rules in respect of her food, dress and habits. The peasant and labour women do not get wages equal to their husbands on account of the fear of society. They are even haunted by punishment here on this earth and elsewhere in hell after death for breach of their duty towards the husband. Thus, she is in eternal slavery without any knowledge whatsoever that she is subjected to inequality and violence. The right to vote is given to her. In many instances the husband decides how it should be cast. In respect of the right to succession, guardianship, divorce etc., her rights have been violated as she is treated as a second class citizen. As per law, equality is proclaimed. But it eludes her grasp in reality. She has no financial security. As most of the women of the middle class do not have the ability, capacity and education to take up jobs, they have to suffer insults and torments in the hands of their husband. The position of a divorced Muslim woman is deplorable. It is horrible and beyond description. All these conditions reduce women in general to the position of a slave and deprive them from the actual enjoyment of their rights.

Women's rights have been violated through centuries all over the world. According to government statistics 18 rapes are committed in the country everyday. But according to unofficial reports a very large number of rape cases go unreported. Along with that, cases of dowry deaths, eve teasing and molestation of women have risen abnormally during the last few years. Unfortunately social attitude towards the victims of such cases is negative. It creates serious psychological problems. People look down upon a victim of rape, whereas a woman who has gone through such a traumatic experience needs social and emotional support. This is a double victimization – one by the rapist and the other by her own social circles. A heartening trend in recent years has been the boldness of victims in raising an outcry against the wrong committed. The age old notions against rape victims such as "everything is lost" are myths made up by men so that women may be prevented from exposing the culprit and the crime. That is exactly what a rapist wants – a license for further monstrous atrocities. Sexual assaults seldom bring sympathy for the victims, who are sometimes driven even to the point of suicide. All these conditions seem to apply exclusively to women. Man escapes unblemished. Woman is condemned, shunned and disgraced, and in this type of environment, women are deprived of their rights to get justice.

One may ask here why are women's rights violated? Reasons are many and varied. Women's right to equality was violated because the society sanctioned it and is still tacitly sanctioning the view that women are in fact not equal to men under the patriarchal social paradigm. This is the reason why although many rules have been promulgated to emphasize equality of both the sexes, the laws have not had any noticeable effect on Indian life as such. Hence, attitudes and social dynamics should be changed if laws could have their desired rights. When a woman is raped, she seldom speaks up because the society, instead of accusing the aggressor, often accuses the woman; instead of looking at the violated woman with sympathy, a stigma is attached to her. The very social norm that women need support because they are weak, promotes the notion that women can be violated and the aggressor can go scot-free. Women's rights are violated because although these rights are given to them by courts of law, they are not sanctioned by society. Without social sanction, women's rights cannot be promoted to any desirable degree.

Women's rights are violated at two different levels: at the level of framing of laws and at the level of application of these laws. In the traditional times, when, for example, Manu framed the rules of Hindu social relations, he was working on this presupposition that men and women are not equal and so laws in matters related to women should be stringent and men should be the decisive factor in these matters. When Manu's laws in matters related to women were actually applied in practice, they were applied even more strictly than the spirit of the laws intended because of the social consensus regarding women's status. Similar has been the case in all matters regarding women. The laws were further prejudiced because they were framed by men who laboured under the patriarchal framework.

Even a scanty look at the Indian civilization tells us beyond doubt that women were not accorded their rights at the institutional level. Their rights were violated. At no point in time, whether during Vedic times or during the time of the *smritis* women were accorded their due, but it can also be noticed that women were denied their rights increasingly and progressively from the Vedic to the time of the *smritis*. Vedic woman's status was only comparatively better and the view that the Vedic woman was equal with man needs a careful examination. Vedic society was built around a strongly patriarchal social order. Son was supposed to live his father's legacy and continue the race, whereas the daughter, though enjoyed a comparatively respectable status, her social role was clearly subsidiary to that of her male sibling. Manu's laws only reinforced this patriarchal bias of the Vedas and laid down thoroughly and specifically patriarchal laws in almost every aspect of social life, so much so his laws have come down even to our times with considerable following.

While occasional voices of dissent are heard against the complex system of Manu and the legal system of the country has promulgated several social laws which go directly against the rulings of the *Dharmasastras*, there has not been a complete social revolution to discard Manu's laws in favour of a more equitable and gender balanced socio-religious legal system. This is because while the vulnerable sections like women and the lower castes, who are at the receiving end of Manu's system, have made only occasional revolts against the system because of the religious sanction attached to it and because those sections which are well placed in Manu's system like men and the higher castes have placed their faith in the system even to this day, albeit tacitly. A tacit but clear acceptance of this system is still prevalent in the Hindu social order, especially among its better placed and powerful minority. Studies of well-known sociologists like M.N. Srinivas have shown that several practices related to this system like the rules of untouchability, worship and family life etc., have been given up by this section of the population due to the pressures of modern life like going for a job outside the home. However, how far and how widely attitudes and mental frameworks behind these practices have changed is a matter of debate. I believe that they still persist with stubborn resistance and that is why women's status have not shown any remarkable improvement in our social system when we consider it in totality. In contemporary India, women's rights are accorded to them by our legal system but at the level of application, women's rights are not protected. They are violated due to man's biased and selfish attitudes. There is a tacit agenda among all favoured sections, whether men in the case of gender disparities or the higher castes in the case of casteism, to protect the system to their advantage as far as it goes. Looking at the history of human civilization all over the globe, it is rather certain that such a system cannot have enduring durability. However, many sections in our country still give it their unsaid consent because of the favours it lavishes on them. It is high time that these sections think simultaneously about the deprivations this system imposes on the less privileged sections as the opposite side of the same coin of the favours it guarantees to one section of our population. History again teaches us that it is hardly that the favoured sections themselves come forward to relinquish the favours placed on them so gratuitously by undeserved social norms, chance, or whatever. Hence, the need for the deprived sections like women and the backward castes in the social hierarchy of the Hindu system to unite and defeat this system, not so much by thwarting it in its entirety but only in its several aspects where injustice is given social protection.

Sadly, women themselves give their social consent in so many unsaid agreements to this system in our country. The system of exploitation would not have been as vibrant as it is now if the womenfolk of India had stood against the discriminations and injustices together as one big chunk of the social space without whose cooperation normal life in society could not have been lived. Women brought up their daughters inscribing in their minds the notion of subservience to the male by the words they spoke to them and subtle ways in which social transactions were carried out by them. While this phenomenon was more clearly visible a few years back, this still holds sway in a surprisingly substantial portion of Indian families, including those in the urban areas. That speaks the story of our nostalgia for the old and traditional. In the same breath, I must add that this state of affairs does not call for blaming the womenfolk of India. As I have pointed out earlier, it was/is simply not possible for many of them to wear a different thinking cap and think differently about gender relations. As human thoughts are culture and situation conditioned, and as thinking goes on always in the backdrop of a consistent framework and not in isolation, our women, deprived as they are, could not picture themselves in any better light. As more and more awareness is today entering every Indian family on a new order of gender relations, this is the appropriate time to strike at the very root of the patriarchal framework.

The old gender order, however, cannot be done away merely in parts. It has to be done holistically in a sweep. It is not that people are intentionally and deliberately up and against giving women their due. Much of the discrimination goes on quietly in an unseen and unaware manner. Even if no one intentionally violates women's rights, the social, political, economic, legal structures in our society are such that women are given a raw deal because disparities are built into the very structure of society. The healing step, I believe, should come first of all from the social sphere because this is the fundamental space where gender relations are defined, taught and handed down. For example, let us consider a scenario in which certain gender sensitive political party gives more tickets for women contestants in election to the Indian Parliament. While this is a positive political step by the party, it can have any effect only if the social dynamics of the constituency accept the bold step. Other parties in that constituency may be asking men to contest and they may win as well due to the subtle gender dynamics in the society. Ultimately the progressive political party may have to rethink its strategy of sending in a woman candidate because of the pressures of party politics and the desire to win. Hence, social dynamics are the primary decisive agents and they have to be the ones to be changed first if any gender equity were to come to stay in our society.

It may be pointed out that the culture and civilization of a country is judged by the rights, respect and status it accords to its women. Ever since independence, Indian women have been given special attention in the various development schemes of the country with a view to bringing them into the national mainstream.[23] We have witnessed an influx of laws for the benefit of women during the post-independence period. Even our constitution makes a number of special provisions for the welfare of women. It is to be noted that under article 15(3), the state has to be empowered to make provisions for the welfare of women. We find that the directive principles of state policy enumerate special provisions for the benefit of women and for the betterment in their social and economic rights. Similarly, under article 51-A, it is the fundamental duty of every citizen to renounce practices derogatory to the dignity of women. It may be pointed out that by taking these constitutional mandates and directives into consideration, many laws have been enacted during the past few years for the welfare of women. There are laws particularly made for women and there are general laws with special provisions for the benefit of women. However, in spite of all this, the plight of Indian woman is not very happy.

It would be worthwhile to mention here that our government set up a national committee in 1971 but the committee which submitted its report in 1974 found that the role of women in India had not improved as was popularly believed. Women's position remained unequal in every sphere of national life. However, the present National Commission for Women (1990), which took shape after 15 years of deliberations by women's associations, is a welcome step. A glance at the functions of the commission shows that it has the power to study, investigate and review all matters relating to the safeguards provided for women under the constitution and other laws. The commission will take up cases of violation and non-implementation of laws enacted to provide protection for women.

As a matter of fact, women in our country enjoy an enviable set of rights constitutionally, compared to women in other countries. Years of experience has shown us that there is no dearth of laws in our country. But what is lacking is proper implementation of these laws.

In fact, women account for just a little less than half of the population of India, but they are not important constituents in decision-making positions in the government, the media, the academia or traditional development agencies. Consequently, while women, especially the poor majority, often bear the brunt of the chronic problems which beset the country and, in addition, carry other burdens related to the gender-based divisions of labour and the general devaluation of women by society. They rarely make it to centre stage in the nation's affairs.[24] India is the second largest country in the world in terms of population and actually more girls are born than boys in this country. However, more girls die compared to boys and the life expectancy at birth is lower for them. As a result there is an unfavourable trend in the sex-ratio. It is an irony that though science has progressed and health facilities have improved, women continue to die. It should be noted that it is proved all over the world that the females have better survival rates. The females are imbued by nature with greater resilience and have a better chance of survival than the male. Sex ratio in advanced countries overwhelmingly favours women. It all proves that our women are allowed to die by neglect as children and adults in this country. This is through malnutrition, lack of health care and general neglect. Right from womb to the tomb, discrimination and exploitation is evident. Though medically the technique known as amniocentesis is used to detect serious mental and physical abnormalities in unborn babies, in reality, the device is misused to get rid of an unwanted daughter. It should be noted that the Medical Termination of Pregnancy Act does not permit such sex selective abortions.

It would be worthwhile to mention here that the Dowry Prohibition Act was passed in 1961 and amended twice in 1984 and 1986, but the machinery for its implementation is yet to be devised. Dowry is a social evil in our society which causes tremendous suffering to women. The dowry prohibition laws have not been very effective in eradicating this evil. Another form of exploitation of women is the practice of child marriage. Inspite of laws against it, child marriages continue. Child Marriage Restraint Act 1929 and 1978 have been unable to prevent the incidence of child marriages in India. Early marriage leads to early motherhood and death, weak children, early widowhood and in innumerable cases, abandonment of wives by the husbands when they grow up and acquire a status. Hindu Succession Act of 1956 has not been able to bring about equality between men and women. Despite the Equal Remuneration Act, 1976 discrimination in wages of men and women continues. Writ petitions filed by aggrieved lady petitioners before various courts including the Supreme Court are a pointers to this effect. The Maternity Benefits Act, 1961 instead of granting maternity leave to women, discourages employers to employ women. In this regard, the most unfortunate thing is that the government itself is one of the greatest violators of the Equal Remuneration Act, 1976. It is well known that the female labourers are paid less than their male colleagues even under government contracts. As a matter of fact, the Government, being the largest employer of women, should ensure that regulations relating to maternity benefits, provisions of crèches at its work sites and wage fixations are adhered to. In our society, sexual abuse and exploitation of women are common things. The increased attention to women and women's issues in the media in the last decade has not been free of blatant sexism and or subtle distortions, partly as a consequence of overt biases and partly due to the very structure of the media. Women's issues are usually not the stuff of what headlines are made. When they do draw the attention of the media they are often sensationalized, trivialized or otherwise distorted. Woman's body is depicted in the media in the most vulgar manner to boost the sale of products and this is in itself a most serious atrocity against women. There are laws against it but they are not effective. Prostitution is another form of exploitation of women. This, however, is not banned but only regulated in our country through legislations. In matrimony a wife occupies a backseat, exceptions apart. She suffers indignities and cruelties. If the marriage crumbles, she has to move out of the family, shelterless and penniless. The society views her with suspicion. There are laws which give her right to seek maintenance but for that, she has to languish in courts. She has no right over the matrimonial house she has built over the years. Even today a woman in Indian society has no value outside the institution of marriage.

It would be worthwhile to mention here that we have become puffed up in the arrogance of our education and civilization. We lecture everywhere about *Swatantrata* (independence/ freedom), but even in our dreams we cannot conceive of the fact that the bud of national independence and civilization must first awaken in the characters of that nation's individuals. How each parent treats his/her daughter or men their mothers, sisters and wives, tells us about that nation's civilization and progress. But if any other nation penetrates into our lives what will it say about the shameful things that exist in most of the families in our society, such as quarrels between fathers and sons, between brothers, all sorts of tensions within families? What will happen to our arrogance about our civilization and education? It must be noted here that whenever we talk of correcting the wrongs of Indian women and establishing their equality with men, many of us refer to the scripture and speak of their status as the goddess (*Devi*). But where do we see any respect for this goddess?

It must be pointed out here that woman was not created to be the ignorant slave or the plaything of man. As it is the purpose of women's life to do good to others, and to live for them, so does a woman live for herself and the serious responsibilities that are entrusted to her demand not only a sympathetic heart, but also a cultivated head. As a matter of fact, one of the main reasons for the non-implementation of laws regarding women is that on the one hand, women lack adequate knowledge about the existence of any such laws and on the other hand, majority of women are deprived of their rights, are poor and therefore unable to avail of the existing legal provisions. That is why most of the commissions and organizations established in the past have been beyond the reach of ordinary women.

The vast majority of women in India are illiterate, underpaid, exploited and deprived. The Indian women have to survive in complex socio-cultural, historical, political and economic contexts. Our society takes women for granted or to be tortured or 'commoditized'. There can be no two opinions that women today can no longer be regarded as the weaker sex and discriminated against as second class citizens. Brutal customs like Sati, child marriage, dowry, unbearable widowhood, polygamy of men, denial or re-marriage to widows etc., should be done away with and women should be allowed to lead a life of dignity.

Therefore, we can say that the main reason behind the violation of rights of women are deprivation or lack of education, lack of their social and political awakening, lack of training in self defence to protect themselves from exploitation, lack of participating in administration, in legislatures, lack of awareness of their position as slaves, lack of awareness of their miserable condition, lack of awareness of their mental slavery, feeling of inferiority to men, lack of cultivating a scientific outlook coupled with a spirit of modernism, and a lack of developing a philosophy of life based on rationalism.

It can be said that women in the Indian social setup can be described as the victims of their own 'diseased psyches' in which they perceive themselves as incompetent and helpless creatures, looked down upon by significant others in their lives. Lucky are those few women who have overcome these psychological barriers and evolved successful strategies for coping up with hostile circumstances and forces in the personal, familial and social environment. It would, therefore, be in the fitness of things if consistent efforts are made today not only to study and analyse the psychology of women folk at different stages of life in working and non-working environments but also to scientifically study the strategies evolved by the successful few who have been able to break the age old myths about women's helplessness, incompetence, lack of drive and motivation to reach pinnacles of glory. A great effort is required to provide women folk with necessary psychological security, nurturing, support, guidance and counseling to enable them to understand themselves in more realistic and progressive terms. Today when we are all thinking of ways and means to break the barriers that stand in the way of women's progress let one thing be clear that women alone can break the barriers they and their society have created for themselves over centuries.

REFERENCES

1. Indira J. Parikh and Pulin K. Garg, *Indian Women : An Inner Dialogue* (New Delhi: Sage Publications, 1989)
2. E. E. Maccoby and C. N. Jackline, *The Psychology of Sex Differences* (Stanford: Stanford University, 1974)
3. Ernest R. Hilgard, Rita I. Atkmson and Richard C. Atkinson, *Introduction to Psychology* (New York: Harcourt Brace Javano Inc., 1953)
4. Leen I. Tyler, *Psychology of Human Differences* (n.p: Vakils Feffer and Simons Private Ltd., 1965)
5. Benett et all "Men and Women: Personality Patterns and Concepts," *Genet Psychology Monograph*, 1959

6. I. E. Tyler, "The Antecedents of Two Varieties of Interest Patterns," *Genet Psychology Monograph*, 1964
7. L.M. Walter and S.S. Marzolf, "The Relation of Sex: Age and School Achievement to Levels of Aspiration", *Journal of Educational Psychology*, 1964
8. M. Horner, "Sex Differences in Achievement Motivation and Performance in Competitive and Non-competitive Situations" (Unpublished Doctoral Dissertation, University of Michigan, 1968)
9. S. Singh and R. Kapoor, "Some Correlates of Projective Measures of Motive to Avoid Success in Males and Females," *British Journal of Projective Psychology and Personality Study*, 1982
10. R.M. Oetzel, *Selected Bibliography on Sex Differences*, Stanford University (Mimeographed), 1962
11. J. I. Blueman, *The Social Institution of Occupational Segregation*, Sign I, Part 2, 1976
12. S. Rothman, *Women's Proper Place: A History of Changing Ideas and Practices, 1870 to the Present* (New York: Basic Books, 1973)
13. J. B. Miller, *Towards a New Psychology of Women* (Baston: Beacon Press, n.y)
14. A.S. Northby, "Sex Differences in High School Scholarship," *School and Society*, 86, 1958
15. A. K. Gupta and S. K. Sharma, "Academic Achievement as Function of Sex, Socio-economic Status, Family Size and Family Type," *Journal of Education*, The Rajasthan Board, July-December, 1982
16. E. M. Terman and L.E. Tyler, "Psychological Sex Differences," I. Carmichael, ed., *Manual of Child Psychology*, 2nd Edition (New York: Wilay, 1954)
17. G. W. Allport, P. F. Verman and G. Lindzey, "Composite Psychographs of Adult Men and Women on the Allport Verman Study of Values," *Study of Values* (Baston: Houghton Miffin, 1951)
18. N.Y. Reddy, *Values and Attitudes of Indian Youth: A Psychological Study of Rural and Urban Students* (n.p: Light and Life Publishers, 1980)

19. R.G. Bernrentes, "The Theory and Construction of the Personality," *Social Psychology*, 1933

20. A. H. Maslow, "Self Actualization and Beyond," in J.F.T. Bugental, ed., *Challenges of Humanistic Psychology* (New York: McGraw Hill, 1967)

21. E. H. Erickson, *Childhood and Society*, 2nd Edition (New York: Norton, 1963)

22. E.H. Erickson quoted in Ram Kumar V., *Self Concept and Achievement* (Trivandrum: Radha Publications, 1975)

23. See *Yojana*, Vol.35, No.22, December 15, 1991, p.17

24. See *Economic and Political Weekly*, Vol.XXVI, No.43, October 26, 1991, p.75

6

Protection and Promotion of the Right of Women

The attitude of ancient society towards women was conditioned by the nature of rights and privileges given to them. It was natural that such a symbol of auspiciousness and an object of affection was to be given sufficient protection of rights by the society and the family. It was also essential for guarding their chastity as well. Of such importance was the protection of a maiden that the kings were ordained, despite their multifarious duties, to protect them. Perhaps this protection which was a social duty of the king was given to those maidens who were orphans. It was, however, the duty enjoined upon a father to protect his daughter. But it appears that they had also great independence in their father's homes. It is really surprising how Kunti of the Great Epic could hide the fact of her pregnancy and if her parents knew about it, one might suppose in the spirit of the Epic that perhaps they would not have minded. The son of a maiden according to later didactic portions was considered a disgrace. Even in Kunti's case, it might have been so as she abandoned her child and had a sense of guilt throughout her life. But there was in existence another social standard according to which one did not mind such incidence.

Krishna states that those conversant in scriptures

recognized Karna as *Kanina* or the legitimate son of his mother's husband. He was even ready to coronate Karna, in case he agreed. Vyasa, himself a *Kanina*, does not deplore the circumstances of Karna's birth. From the conversation between Sarmishtha and Devayani, we may well infer that Devayani was only worried lest the father of Sarmishtha's children turn out to be *Yayati*. Otherwise there was no restriction on the maidens and they could have *Kanina* sons through *Brahmana rshis*, without knowing their lineage. The lists of sons in the Great Epic – however repugnant the custom may be today – show that the society of the time was a free one. There was no downright or perpetual condemnation attached to anyone for no fault of her own. The sins of parents were not vested upon the children and thus Vysa, a *Kanina*, was greatly revered. Nevertheless, it cannot be assumed that fathers were always careless about the duty of protection of their daughter's virtue. In the Great Epic, according to another story, Agni loved King Nila's daughter and was accepted by her. One day in the guise of a *Brahmana* he was enjoying the pleasure of that maiden's company. The virtuous king on the discovery of the truth punished the *Brahmana* according to the law. This clearly indicates that such relations were forbidden by laws. The maiden's innocent activities were, however, not restricted. They used to go to gardens for sports, and sometimes were courted by lovers when they were out for pleasure. Mixed parties were arranged at Raivataka mountain and it was on her way back from such a party that Subhadra was abducted.

The attitude of society towards women determines her property and legal rights. Therefore, such rights of maidens state that generally after marriage, except in the case of *Putrika*, the daughter had nothing to do with her parental home and property. An unmarried daughter, however, had the right to inherit her mother's dowry. The liberty enjoyed by women and its gradual deterioration will also indicate the attitude of society towards women. The life long protection due to the physical weakness of women may have been imposed for their benefit. If a woman lost all her protectors, it was the duty of the king to protect her. With such protection no idea of tutelage, confinement, seclusion or restriction to their freedom was associated. The family and the royal protection, in fact, gave them liberty of movement.

It has been stated that it was only in a kingless country that amorous men were not able to accompany women in the woods. If the king protected well, it is said, women and maidens decked with ornaments could fearlessly wander everywhere without male relatives to attend upon them. The Epic societies were mostly monarchical. This goes to establish that the movements of women were in no way restricted. Women attended courts for business. They moved freely in public particularly on festive occasions or for witnessing any strong object or event. On the occasion of Krishna's arrival at Hastinapura on his peace mission and when the Pandavas went out in the coronation procession, the houses were so thronged with women that they were on the point of falling. Even in the republics of the *Vrshis* and *Andakas*, it will be shown presently, that the ladies of aristocratic families used to attend festivals with the commoners.

From the narrative part of the Epics, it is clear that the movements of the ladies of the inner apartments were not much confined. They followed their husbands to forests, wars and hunting expeditions. Some of them like Satyawati, Ambika and Ambalika went for penances even without any male protection. Sometimes they went to the woods to visit *Rshi* families. They appeared before assemblies and were coroneted in public.

The ladies of royal families had their outdoor pleasure also. Subhadra was abducted when she was returning after attending the public festival at Raivataka. The *Vrshni* and *Andhaka* ladies often attended these festivities. The *Kuru* ladies went out to the forest for picnics and for visiting their relations. The inner apartment built in one of the excursions was just to keep these ladies from the public gaze so that they could freely dance, sing, laugh, drink and sport in water. Sita went with Sugriva's wives to show them the city of Ayodhya. It has been already stated that the ladies attended *Swayamvaras*, funerals and tournaments. Queens sometimes had to forgo their modesty and drew chariots for the *Brahmanas* which would be unthinkable in the *purdah* system. In grief, also, all modesty was thrown to the winds.

Despite all this freedom certain manners and passages in the Epics indicate that the custom of seclusion of women was prevalent. Rama's opinion that during calamities, wars, *Swayamvaras*, sacrifices and marriages there was no fault if women appeared unveiled, especially with their husbands, suggests that this was not otherwise encouraged. It may be that even on the above mentioned occasions married ladies appeared with their husbands, i.e., their protectors. Lakshmana had an objection to looking at Sita in the absence of Rama. Mandodari's lamentations indicate that the *Rakshasa* chief did not like his wife's coming out unveiled. Draupadi appeared properly veiled before Narada. Her lamentations in the court of the Kuru's prove that the Kuru ladies were not accustomed to appear before an assembly. Some descriptions point to the fact that these ladies never appeared before a crowd, they were not even seen by the sun or the wind. Among the young ladies of the royal household, it was not a custom to talk to strangers and in case it was absolutely necessary a blade of grass was placed by them in between. It was perhaps a symbolic curtain showing the limits of which were not to be transgressed.

All the seclusion, life outside the palaces, enjoyments, political missions, visiting and living in the forests, does not prove that there was *purdah* system, confinement or restriction of freedom, all of which developed later on. The royal ladies kept aloof from the commoners, who sometimes include unwanted and uncultured persons among their crowds. Thus their seclusion was a sign of respectabilities. It was meant merely to guard their chastity, to which great importance was attached by later societies depicted in the Epics, for their chastity guarded purity of their lord's royal-race as well as his property and kingdom. It is primarily due to this reason that the system of 'harems' may have been followed by the propertied classes, although to a lesser extent it may have been prompted to check palace conspiracies and revolutions.

The duties of the maidens go along with their rights. The duties of the maidens at home were mostly for preparing them for their future career, i.e., the domestic life. The greatest duty of a house-holder was to entertain guests. As a practical part of their education, daughters performed this duty at their parental homes. Sakuntala offered seat, water and '*Arghya*' to Dushyanta while her foster father was absent. Kunti entertained and pleased sage Durvasa. She not only saved her father from a difficult situation but also received a boon for herself. Sanjaya ordered his daughter Sukumari to look after the guests – Narad and Parvata. The daughters of poor people might have helped their fathers with the boats. They had duties on the ceremonial occasions, of welcoming the guests.

Like Kunti others also saved their fathers or their race from difficult situations. Sarmishtha, although a princess, readily became a slave, for the departure of Sukracharya would have been a great calamity for the Asura kingdom. Although Lopamudra's father hesitated, she herself consented to marry the poor Agastya in order to save her father from that *Rshi*'s curse. Sukanya did not utter a word of opposition when she was given away to the old blind *rshi* Chyarana Jaratkaru who toiled like a slave to save the race of the *Nagas*. This self-sacrificing spirit, an essential factor in harmonious family relations, was inculcated in maidens through the education they received at home. Their education was in keeping with their place as well as their secular and religious activities at home.

From the accounts of the heroines it appears that the responsibility of educating the daughters was fully realized by the parents but there is little corroborative evidence. The epics being hero-centred present no data of this kind. However, the fact cannot be denied that the Epic heroines were highly educated. Draupadi has been mentioned as *Pandita* and *Brahmavadini* (and so are Oghavat and Arundhati). Her advice to Yudhishthira is indicative of her practical wisdom. Draupadi confesses that she had instructions from learned *Brahmanas* who were appointed by her father to instruct her brother on the duties expounded by Brahaspati. When she went out of the inner apartment and sat on her father's lap the learned Brahmanas, recited the sweet and consoling truths to her. Kunti's admonitions to the Pandavas show that she was well instructed in mind and heart, and was fit to be the mother of heroes. Like the parents of today she worried not so much about the safety of her sons, as for their duty and righteous fame. To her their death was better than their parasitical existence. Kunti's advice is fully worthy of a Kshatriya mother of a heroic age.

Certain passages in the Epics prove that the maidens were given Vedic education. Women were able to perform sacrifices alone, even without their husbands. In the *Ramayana*, Kausalya on the eve of Rama's installation offered oblation to fire, reciting 'mantras'. Similarly when Vali was going to fight Sugriva, Tara performed '*swastyayana*' with the chanting of 'mantras' and so also Kausalya when Rama was going to the forest. Women recited daily Vedic prayers (*Sandhaya*). Tara had knowledge of the qualities of speech and of the philosophy of emancipation for the Philosopher Janaka was confuted by her. In the *Mahabharata* there is mention of a learned *Brahmani* who wanted to be enlightened on the mysteries of religion, life and death. Siva, another ascetic woman, was well versed in the Vedas. Even *Rshis*, deities and others went to Arundhati to learn the secrets of religion and duty and were duly instructed by her.

As the Great Epic records, many strata of societies in this period in which religious and philosophical education of the Vedas is mentioned to have been imparted to women correspond roughly with the Upanishad and the Sutra period. These works contain enough evidence of the intellectual activities and educational attainments of women. Draupadi's lively discussion reminds one of Gargi and Maitreyi of *Brhadaranyaka Upanishad*. *Aswalayana Grhyasutra* records *Samavartana* ceremony for the girls. There were girls' schools and learned women when Panini wrote *Ashtadhyayi*. *Paraskara Grhyasutra* narrates 'mantras' to be uttered by a mother. True, the mere fact that these women could recite 'mantras' does not warrant the conclusion that they had a knowledge of the Vedas. The claim rests on ampler evidence. In the commentary on *Gobhila Brhya-Sutra* we are told: "the women folk should be taught, for without such study they cannot perform *Agnihotra*." And *Agnihotra* was definitely performed by the ladies in the epics. Kausalya could quote from a *Dharmasutra*.

It seems that when the epics were first being written the conservative attitude of the *Dharmasutras* had not gained ground. Those women who performed penances for the liberation of soul must have had some intellectual and philosophical education. At any rate the fact is undeniable that they had excellent mental training. The austerities performed by Amba and Anusuya were beyond the capacities of many *Rshis*. A hermitage near Kurukshetra which was a seat of women ascetics deserves special mention. Her observing the vow of *Brahmacharya* (celibacy) from her young age of *Brahmani* maiden rose to a high point in ascetic eminence. She acquired unusual yogic power and became *Siddha*. While another, not a child of poverty but of affluence, the daughter of King Sandilya, self-restrained, wedded to serve vows, performed austerities, usually too hard to be accomplished by women. On the basis of merits thus acquired she obtained a place in heaven, and was worshipped by the Gods and *Brahmanas*. Dira and Swayamprabha had taken the vow of celibacy, i.e., *Brahmacharya* and were living as ascetics. Saamani Sabri used to put on barbs and skin of antelope and had been described as "*Jatila Tapasi*" with her *asrama* at Pampa and with Matanga, her late preceptor. In the Epics we come across such words as '*Bhikshunis*', '*paravrajita*' and '*tapaswini*', which clearly point to the fact that the women too practised asceticism and performed penances. Penances were sometimes performed with some worldly object in view. Nevertheless, these examples also indicate that women had considerable mental discipline and physical endurance which would compare well with similar attainments of their male counterparts. Conditions changed when the time the didactic portions of the *Mahabharata* were being written. Religious as well as literary education was not imparted to girls. Women were considered incompetent to perform sacrifices. There are also clear indications that women were not given literary education.

With increased emphasis on *pativrata dharma* chastity assumed greater importance. In order to keep women perfectly chaste, their movements have been restricted gradually in the later times as depicted in Mahabharata, due to lack of education and therefore loss of intellectual activity and rational thinking. Women became ignorant. Child marriages and thus living in an unsympathetic atmosphere from an early age with ignorant mothers-in-law and co-wives might have developed a jealous temperament among women and deteriorated their character. Most of them having no other interest in life might have imbibed luxurious habits, fickle and vile character which was exaggerated by the school of renunciation to carry propagation against women. It was stated that due to their fickle character women were to be guarded carefully throughout their lives. The theory of perpetual tutelage and complete dependence on men, an outcome of ignorance, was responsible for fetters that chained women for ages to come.

However, this hackneyed portrait of Indian woman has been gradually transformed and a new Indian woman is now born. We shall see how important social values and social attitudes are responsible for making social legislation a success.[1] Law can be a powerful force for social change only if a large majority of people favour the new social norms.[2] As an instrument of social change, the law involves two interwoven processes. New enactments such as the Hindu Code Bill institutionalized a new pattern of behaviour, manifesting new social values.

When this new pattern was incorporated in the legal code any deviation from this pattern was punished according to law. But institutionalization by itself is not enough for a law to become an active social force. There should be a correlated cultural process for the internalization of this new pattern of behaviour in the individual.[3] All the social legislations enacted by the Government of India have undoubtedly been responsible for transforming of Indian woman from her position of subservience to an equal status with men. Legally there is now no restriction on Indian woman regarding marriage, divorce, property inheritance or any other inequalities. (up to here)

In the absence of internalization of new values, simple institutionalization may bring legislation itself into contempt and women may lose respect for law. For example, from the current Indian situation we can exemplify the relationship between codification and internalization. Before the enactment of the Hindu Code Bill, though polygamy was allowed[4], most Hindus were monogamous, and in fact very few married a second time while the first wife was living. But when the social reformers sought to bring about a change, there was opposition from the orthodox; however, when the act was passed there was acquiescence because there was really no change in social norms. The fear of the orthodox section that women would seek permission in large numbers from courts for judicial separation or divorce did not materialize since the prevailing social norm is against a wife's seeking divorce. Another point that supports this argument is that though according to the Hindu Code Bill marriage is only a contract and could be registered as a civil action, actually the religious customs associated with it have not been given up. So a wife still looks upon her marriage as a sacrament. She would not like to annul it unless her relatives consent. But her relatives would be reluctant to consent because the prevailing social attitudes are very important in making all social legislation a success.[5]

Indian women do not suffer legal disparities but they suffer from practical disparities which continue to exist in the absence of internalization of the institutionalized laws. To bring about social change, change of attitude is very important. Once this is achieved a society will be receptive to ideas to accommodate both modernity and tradition. Practices that serve no useful purpose will be given up.

As has been observed in a study conducted by Rama Mehta, more than education making elders feel comfortable in the new value system, it brought about a fast change in the status of women in Oswal families in the former state of Mewar. These families had been very close to the Maharaja and looked after the administration. When the state joined the Indian union, the Oswals lost their status. They had to go out and compete outside their state as well. Increased education opportunities helped the Oswal men to find good jobs and also educate their women. The old tradition loving

Oswal community transformed itself because the institution of change had been internalized – the old and the new were meshed, each supporting the other.[6] A meaningful change in the role of women can be brought about by the laws with greater ease if women feel confident that the caste-community/ society will support and strengthen their role.

The Hindu Marriages Validity Bill was discussed from 1949.[7] The bill was moved by Pandit Thakur Das Bhargava (East Punjab General). He said that the bill to enable marriages between Hindus, Sikhs, Jains and their different castes and sub-castes was valid. The select committee consisted of Giani Gurmukh Sing Musafir, Sardar Hukam Singh, M. Ananthasayanam Ayyangar, Deshhandhu Gupta, Durgabai Deshmukh, Renuka Ray, Ram Nath Goenka, Bakshi Tek Chand, Lala Achint Ram, Choudhry Ranbir Singh, Mahabir Tyagi and the mover of the bill.[8] It could meet when only five members were present.

Till 1949 a marriage between persons belonging to different castes was not valid. Bombay was, however, an exception as marriages there had an indefinite position. In Punjab unions between Hindu and Sikhs were held valid by society in general but not by courts. Previous to this there were no marriages between Hindus and Jains. A marriage between a Jain Aggarwal and a Hindu Aggarwal is now a possibility. According to the bill of 1946, marriages between members of the sub-division of the principal castes of the Hindus were declared legal in some places and illegal in another. Inter-caste and inter-religious marriages were not legal and it was proposed to be made so. But it was more important to mobilize public opinion first.

Members who favoured this bill said that by making such marriages legal the bitterness of one caste against another would be removed. They referred to the Arya Marriage Validity Act 1938 according to which a Hindu could marry any Hindu outside his caste. The Special Marriage Act of

1872 made it possible for a Hindu to contract such a marriage, provided he declared he would no more be a Hindu. This was the condition under the non-amended bill. An Act of 1923 provided that if a person wanted to marry outside his religion under the Amendment Act "their previous rights are unaffected to the extent provided in the Caste Disabilities Removal Act." Such couples were to lose the right of inheritance.

A member drew attention to the political consolidation carried out by Sardar Patel and said it was important to do the same on the social front. Such a step would lessen communal tension and help in consolidating Hindu society. Although educated people married out of their caste, they encountered great difficulty and bitter criticism.

The bill was supported by Mahvir Tyagi (VP General) who said "India has suffered on account of communal differences. Marriages are the root cause and the elections the fruit cause for all these differences. Every time marriages take place caste is enquired into. The next occasion for enquiring about caste is when a person stands for election." The bill was favoured by many members and the motion was finally adopted.[9] But debates continued for long on the Special Marriage Bill. Members of the council of states discussed the bill. Muslims as a community were against the bill, though some Muslim members of the select committee supported the measure. The bill was only a permissive measure and not compulsory. The committee was unable to come to any conclusion on the question of religion. Even in May 1954 there was an inconclusive debate on the Special Marriage Bill.

Maya Devi Chetty (Congress – West Bengal) said that in case of marriages between parties of different religions the woman should adopt the religion of her husband to avoid troubles. Mona Hensman (Congress – Madras) said that by granting the right on inter-religious marriages the bill would uphold the constitution and the secular laws of the state. She said the bill gave the blessing of monogamy, of which divorce was a corollary. Her experience was that among the communities which had the right to divorce only a few had exercised it. She said that the three year period given to husband and wife would give them time to make adjustments. Shyamala I Rao of New Delhi said in a letter to the editor to *The Statesman* that both houses of the parliament had passed the Special Marriage Bill after an interesting debate. This was supposed to be a progressive, permissive and experimental measure. According to Nehru, it was the first step towards bringing about a certain uniformity in India, removing the barriers of caste, society and religion. It was a significant improvement on the old act. It provided for recognition of illegitimate children and thus unrecognized unions were to be legalized. It gave full freedom to persons who wanted to marry outside their caste, province or religion. Another letter deplored the provision for divorce in the bill. The aims of the bill were new to conservative Indian society which attached the greatest importance to customs and traditions and so there was great opposition to it.

The Act provides for marriage between two adults of different religions or castes but of the age of 21 and 18 years for males and females, respectively. This also serves as a check on child marriage and registration of marriages is compulsory under section 16 of the Act, which allows voluntary registration of marriages celebrated under other laws.

It appears that we as people have not properly understood the idea behind registration of marriages. They still consider it a disgrace. It would be available if all marriages were registered as this is the only proof that a marriage has been solemnized. Parsees criticized the Bill feeling it would create hardships as it prohibited certain degree of relationship. Muslims also criticized it as did Christians. Some of its provisions appear very harsh, such as a Hindu marrying under it will be deemed to have separated from his family. Regarding inheritance and succession it went according to the Hindu Succession Act.

The act makes it clear that contemplated special marriages can only be monogamous. Moreover, marriages performed under it do not compel the parties concerned to declare their religions. Although inter-caste, inter-religious and inter-regional marriages have been legalized by the Special Act 1954, public opinion is generally not favourable to it. Of these three kinds of marriages, inter-relational unions are less criticized than the other. If a Brahman boy from Bombay marries a Brahman girl from Andhra or any other state, society will still accept the marriage because it is between two Brahmans.

Inter-caste marriages are still criticized despite the fact that many have married and are marrying outside their caste. This creates a problem for such couples as they become victims sometimes of society and sometimes of their own relatives. Social criticism is, however, less torturous as people other than the relatives of the couple will be quiet after months or after a few years at the most. The worst critics are relatives who will do their best to humiliate the couples. Inter-caste couples adjust themselves very well but their relatives are not happy. They tell these young people that they have brought a bad name to the family by their shameless deeds. Social pressure works against such marriages. There is nothing inherently bad in an inter-caste marriage. Harm lies in an educated girl liking a boy and deciding to marry him because she feels that she would be happier with him rather than with a boy of her own caste. In 90 percent or more cases parents discourage their daughters from marrying boys not of the same caste. In the remaining cases, where parents give due consideration to the happiness of their daughters and give their consent, they too became victims. Elders who believe themselves wise will not leave them alone.

They will talk in sarcastic ways and say that their daughter had no regard for the family's reputation. Stress is more on daughters because they and their parents have to face the consequences. The sacrifice the parents made to see their children happy goes unnoticed. In other inter-caste marriages the parents of girls agree, but it is the other members of the family whose attitude spoil everything and such girls go in for court (civil) marriages. Parents who arrange such marriages deserve the sincere gratitude of their children, because it is this particular kind of parents who think of nothing but their daughter's happiness. Inter-caste couples should remember to give due regard to their parent's throughout, for had their parents, brothers and sisters not supported them they would not have been able to marry in a happy atmosphere. Where parents do not agree, marriages are solemnized but a great deal of mental tension is there.

Rita Sharma's article "Inter-caste couples – victims of prejudice" is a pointer to the criticism and prejudice that await these couples. Out of six women she interviewed all talked about estrangement of relation between them and their parents as a result of inter-caste marriage. Since the parents did not agree to their marriage they were either arranged by friends or by political parties where their husbands were working. These couples have faced financial problems and have had great difficulties in settling down in life. They were again helped by their friends and not their parents. The parents felt that they were not responsible for their hardships, that they would have been married to economically well off husbands had they listened to them. This is the usual excuse of parents of girls who marry against their wishes. The women interviewed feel that leaving aside the financial problem they were happy because their husbands loved them and they did not hurt their feelings. The number of such couples is quite big. The problem arises because of tradition, customs and rituals matter more to our society. Some couples face problems because they marry in a hurry. In most instances the husband is employed, but if he is not living becomes difficult. Failure of love marriages is at best equal to, if not less than, that of arranged marriages. Reconciliation of both the parental families would help such couples a great deal.[10]

The Medical Termination of Pregnancy Act was passed in 1971. It provides for ending the pregnancy of a girl below 18 years without her consent so long as her guardian's consent is obtained.[11] The medical termination of pregnancy act of 1971 has legalized abortion. An abortion is permitted if continuance of pregnancy involves risk to the life of the mother or to her physical or mental health. Pregnancy caused by rape or by the failure of a contraceptive device (in case of a married woman) can also be terminated. If there is a substantial risk that a child if born will be seriously handicapped either physically or mentally abortion is permitted. The pregnancy of a woman below the age of 18 cannot be terminated without the consent of her guardians given in writing. Consent of the husband does not appear to be necessary when a married woman requires an abortion. This Act has given the right to Indian women to limit their families. It is good if after one such voluntary abortion husband or wife goes in for vasectomy or tubectomy, respectively. Termination of pregnancy would then serve a meaningful purpose. It would be of little help if after one goes for several abortions because the law permits it. It is the duty of a woman who undergoes it once to make some arrangement which will prevent an unwanted conception.

The Act helps women only if it is properly used. While MTP has legal sanction and if properly used could help Indian women, another trend is noticed among urban middle class women to undergo sex test (pre-birth sex determination). Despite the centre's instructions to the state governments, these tests are performed and consequent scientific female feticide is back in contemporary India because when the tests reveal the presence of a female foetus women go in for abortion. This endangers the lives of women because tests are carried out after four months of conception. Sex tests must be banned by the government. Otherwise at the rates these test are becoming popular it will increasingly become difficult for the female child to be born.[12]

In hospitals there is to a great extent less misuse. Doctors want women who want the termination of pregnancy to bring their husbands to sign before this is done and also perform vasectomy or tubectomy. Some doctors in private clinics who are after money do not mind aborting as many times as a married woman wants. They also do not hesitate to perform the MTP operation on unmarried girls. It would be better if doctors see to the proper implementation of this Act and save women from harming their health on account of heavy bleeding because of abortion and other side effects. Doctors should not perform such an operation on an unmarried girl (unless she has been forced into sexual intercourse) who goes out to enjoy and then come to the doctor because she or the man who is responsible for her conception can afford to pay a heavy medical bill. She must have the child even without marriage.

Giving and taking dowry is prohibited by law. But the law is totally ineffective and is flouted every day with impunity since no party to giving dowry cares to lodge a police complaint. Parents give dowry to raise the status of their daughters. It is considered a female right to property and they say that a daughter must have something to fall back upon in time of need. Dowry has taken the form of *Kanyadaan*, which used to be the token gift to a daughter, her husband and the in-laws. But dowry has today crossed all bounds. Despite the fact that there is much inflation, there is no decrease in giving and taking of dowry. There is competition between the dowry givers and dowry takers. In case of dowry, weight of social norms is more effective than the legal norms.

Educated girls must bear in mind that their parents have spent much in educating them like the boy's parents. Moreover, these girls earn as much as boys and sometimes even more. So where is the need to take dowry? It is sad that education has hardly had any liberating influence on people in regard to dowry. On the contrary, education has increased this social evil, an all-time nightmare for the parents of a girl.

Since the law has not been properly implemented, dowry can be checked not by legislation but by mobilizing public opinion. Only people of the young generation can check dowry. They should at once check their parents and other relatives who talk of dowry. The Dowry Prohibition Act of 1961 has virtually failed because an infringement of its provision is not made a cognizable offence. The Dowry Act of 1961 only institutionalized the issue; internalization did not follow. The law is flouted because it has a number of loopholes.

Increase in dowry mentally tortures marriageable girls and their families. The fact is that dowry has now become sophisticated; there is a sense of competition in it and parents find it difficult to meet demands. Women have been killed for bringing inadequate dowry. Bride burning, an urban middle class phenomenon, is increasing every day. Despite the cruelties dowry has brought in the lives of educated Indian women, it continues because no social stigma is attached to it. Dowry death was an issue before parliament and the Amendment of the 1961 Act has yet to be finalized. It is wrong to deny dowry death and describe them as a means used by a girl's parents to blackmail and defame a boy's family. Serious efforts to check this phenomenon should not be unnecessarily delayed. Demanding dowry should be a cognizable offence.[13]

When girls are given education by their parents to become working women, it will be taxing the limited resources of their parents to take dowry. The new form of dowry never ends its demands and the expectations continue even after 15 or 20 years of marriage. At least some check can operate if the persons who take or give dowry are punished by law. Further a social stigma should be attached to dowry in all forms.

Women in contemporary India are strong, determined and despite great difficulties go out to work. They need support and the one person that matters to a married woman is her husband and parents to an unmarried girl. Only a few husbands help their working wives; many do not because their ego is hurt when their wives earn. This is irrational and is a complete social construct. Marriage is a complete partnership. When both husband and wife earn and appreciate each other, there is a soothing atmosphere at home. Their life together is strengthened, their children grow up well with independent habits and learn to appreciate their parents.

With the spread of education, women are trying to be both housewives and career women. This is not easy. It is difficult to take care of one's career after marriage. The trend towards relative economic independence of women is accepted by men with an ambivalent attitude. When she is economically helping the family, she is also able to be an asset to the husband, but at no cost must she neglect her traditional household duties.[14] Supportive environment needs to be created for working women in their homes. It is a tendency of in-laws of working women to expect them to do household works as well, not realizing the fact that they too go out to work like their sons. Working women have great difficulties if the husbands ignore their practical problems. Exhausted from work, if working women cannot find breathing space even in their homes, they will be laden with stress.[15]

Even at work women are discriminated. In factories and offices, they are either paid lower wages or employed on low paid jobs. Discrimination is seen even in the professions. Women are ignored for promotion not because they are less intelligent or less hardworking than their colleagues but because they are women. Sex discrimination in work has blocked our country's economic growth and social development too long. Dependents and the uneducated seek employment in agriculture and allied industries, plantation, mining, building and construction industries also provide employment to these women. Some employers employ unmarried girls, on condition that they leave their jobs as soon as they marry.[16] This is decidedly unfair, discriminatory and unjust. The government should see to the enforcement of laws passed by it in this connection.

A study conducted by the labour bureau of the Government of India shows that the number of women in non-agricultural industries is declining. In an article entitled "Status of Women in Industry," E.D'Souza has observed that there is a clear discrimination in wages paid to women. They were and are hired on lower jobs carrying lower wages and there is neither avenue of promotion open to them nor protection of security of employment. The occupation which attracts the maximum number of urban female workers is teaching followed by wage labour.[17]

Although women have hitherto occupied themselves with traditional jobs like teaching, nursing and social work, with the beginning of professional consciousness, they are now seeking various positions in the occupational hierarchy. There has been a gradual switchover in the employment of women from traditional occupations to more remunerative and higher status jobs. They are now taking up such professions as administration, education, medicine, engineering, architecture, town planning, nuclear physics, journalism, community development projects and in many other professions except defence. It is indeed a healthy trend that educated women in India today aspire for a professional career. The increased opportunities for training and education have enhanced their employability. But the opportunities for entering an occupation and progressing in it have not increased proportionately.[18] In the absence of wage paid employment in the recent past, women sought self-employment in the form of domestic industries such as knitting, embroidery, tailoring and pickling. In addition to this, educated women engaged in jobs like freelance journalism, translation, commercial art, fine arts, cartooning and also some unconventional fields like hair-dressing, beautician and tourist guiding. These jobs are becoming popular in bigger cities. It is interesting to discover that such professions for women were unheard of before 1947. Indian society disliked the idea of women working with men in office. It was only after 1943 (first rationing system) and after 1947 that middle class women came out to work in large numbers. Old social prejudices against work are weakening.

In lower and middle class families, women work to supplement their family's income. But in the upper classes, women work mainly to develop their talents and raise their own status. There is still a wide gap in opportunities and facilities available in general to women compared with men. Since 1947 Indian women have been entering the IAS, IFS, Indian Revenue Service, IPS etc., but their number is still very small compared with women in lower posts in offices. Even in industries the number of women in higher posts is smaller if compared with those working in low-paid jobs because of technological change.

The law is on women's side but prejudices, hostilities and resistance and social taboos still hold them back. It is therefore necessary to set up effective machinery for the implementation and enforcement of laws by the government.

A number of women's organizations have been taking a keen interest in the welfare and progress of Indian women. The first and the most important is the All India Women's

Conference founded in 1927. It voices the problems of women. Its objectives are non-political and social. Right from its inception, the Conference has worked to elevate women to the same footing as men. Because of its efforts, public opinion was mobilized in favour of the Hindu Code Bill. The National Council of Women in India, founded in 1925, also works to raise the status of women. It has worked in the area of education, medical facilities and family planning since 1947. Bhartiya Grmeen Mihila Sangh founded in 1955 worked to improve the condition and status of rural Indian women. It has been organizing training courses for women who work on the land as well as *mahila mandals* in villages. The National Federation of Indian Women was founded in 1954. It is different from the other organizations and tries to give Indian women political awareness to fight social injustice. Recent protests by women in different parts of the country against rising prices, hoarding, adulteration and corruption were organized by the federation. Stri Shakti Jagran Movement was organized to mobilize women. It fights for a just place in Indian society. This organization believes in the ideals and methods of Gandhi. It believes that the status of women can be raised by women alone. It appeals to all women to object to *purdah*, untouchability and dowry. The Federation of University Women Association, the All-India Medical Women's Conference and the Trained Nurses Association look in to the interests of teachers and lecturers, doctors and nurses while the Women Lawyers' Association looks in to the interests of women in the legal profession. Trade unions work for the welfare of women workers.

The transformation of Indian women has been brought about to a great extent today. The forces that have helped in the emergence of new women in India have been a number of laws passed by the government and the efforts of these women's organizations. The attitude of the families of working women has changed to such an extent that they do not mind if their daughter-in-law works. They do want her to add to the family income.

The new woman of India would emerge completely when her family learns to respect her feeling, realize that she has worked the whole day like her husband if she is married or like her brother if she is unmarried. The atmosphere at home has to be warm to treat a working woman fairly. This does not imply that only working women need to be treated with love and kindness. In fact all our women are working – some work at home from morning till night while others go out to work after completing their domestic work.

In villages, *panchayats* can do much for the uplift of rural women. *Gram Seviks* and *Mukhya Sevikas* are partners in the effort to build a better community. The village *panchayats* must provide facilities to their women and see that a proper atmosphere and good working conditions exist.

The dynamic women of the country have to formulate a policy and programme for the emancipation of their sisters. Up till now, by and large, lack of self-confidence, initiative and perseverance has contributed to the stagnation of the women's movement in the country. Self-criticism is the need of the hour. A plan of action is to be drawn up with vigour, drive and fervour and pursued. Activity has to be directed towards three fronts. Implementation of beneficial legislation, translation of government promises and declarations into practice and organization of public opinion for further progress should constitute the basic objectives and tasks before the women's movement.

A woman has to be assured the dignity of her person. She has to have full control over her body. It is for her to determine how many children she should give birth to or for that matter to decide whether she should become a mother at all. It is for her to choose to go in for abortion or not. Nobody, not even the husband, has the right to violate her rights. She shall not be abused, beaten, tormented, assaulted or raped. She, and she alone, has the full authority over her life. She is not cattle to be disposed of. She cannot be forced into slavery or prostitution, nor can she be compelled to pay dowry to gain the status of a wife. She has the right, nay the privilege, to become a mother, if she so desires, though unmarried. Her right to motherhood has to be dissociated from marriage.

Married woman is not just 'queen of the home,' she is much more. She is her husband's life-partner. Her sphere of activity cannot be confined to the home nor can her husband's pleasures dictate her tastes and opinions. No doubt she alone can bear children. But it is given to both man and wife to rear children. Both shall aid and assist each other in running the home. She shall not be condemned to do dull and routine work all by herself. Her rights in respect of succession, guardianship, maintenance, adoption and divorce shall not be such as to be discriminatory.

There must be a uniform civil code applicable to all India citizens and to all territories comprising India. In the transition period, personal laws shall be liberalized. Abuses like *talak* have to be done away with. Family courts shall be established to settle disputes between wife and husband with sympathy and consideration. Irretrievable breakdown of marriage and incompatibility of temperament shall become ground for seeking divorce. Separation and divorce must be unilaterally granted. Alimony and maintenance shall be given to a spouse taking into consideration all the relevant factors. The preponderant claims of mothers to the custody and guardianship of children has to be respected. The provision for restitution of conjugal rights has to be taken out from the statute book. The husband has to be prevented from compelling his wife to resign her job and live at his place of residence. Marriage laws have to be amended to protect the rights of woman over her earnings or property acquired with her earnings. The unemployed wife shall have to get, on divorce, half the property acquired during her coverture by the husband. The wife should get at least half of his property if he dies leaving behind children.

The woman shall not be treated as a perpetual ward by the society. An adult woman should have the right and privilege to choose her husband. The Child Marriage Act has to be amended to make all child marriages illegal. The age of consent for marriage and the age of consent for sexual intercourse shall be different. Lastly, the Suppression of Immoral Traffic Act (SITA) shall not be oppressive against women and discriminatory against them. The courts must become ever ready to come to the rescue of a wronged woman. Tardiness, delay and procrastination are defeating the ends of justice. Speedy and summary justice should be provided to hapless and helpless women. The bureaucracy of the Government and the police should treat woman with respect and consideration.

Women's education has to be encouraged in all ways, seats in educational institutions have to be reserved (at least 30 percent to start with) for women as a measure to reverse discrimination. The cultural atmosphere of the society has to be necessarily changed for the betterment of the women's position and status. Perfect equality in relevant context should reign between the sexes. Male chauvinism has to disappear. Treatment of the woman just as a sex symbol or a sex object has to be abhorred. The craze for male child has to be eliminated form the minds of both men and women.

In the economic sphere, several changes become imperative. The disparity in the wages between men and women has to be eliminated. The principle, 'equal pay for equal work' has to be properly applied and monitored. There should be no discrimination against women – as it is at present – in the matter of selection for jobs, training and promotion. In the name of a special gift of nature, it should not be open to employers – private or public – to push women into dull and tedious jobs like those of nurses, primary school teachers, typists, secretaries and ayahs and debar them from other lucrative, prestigious and privileged offices and jobs. The society has to pay, through the government, the woman sufficient salary during the period she is forced to nurse and rear the child in its tender age. The period of maternity leave with pay has to be enlarged. Provision has to be made for maternity leave without pay also. Of course, the demand for all these facilities may not be available for the second child. A scheme of disincentives in the matter of family planning, if not compulsory family planning leading to a limit of one child per family, has to be adopted because it will ultimately benefit women. They will get enough leisure to enable them to obtain excellence in terms of their talents and jobs. They will further be able to participate not only in the social and cultural life of the country but also in its political processes. Reservation of jobs for women is a must. Protective discrimination in the transition period has to be encouraged.

At preset the position of women in politics is deplorable. Their representation in legislature and judicial bodies of the state is far from satisfactory; it is insignificant. Women constitute 50 per cent of the voters and yet there are only 18 women in the Lok Sabha out of 525 members. The representation is as low as 3 per cent. Is it not absurd? Is it safe for democracy? Can it be termed democracy at all when one half of the Indian people – women – are denied adequate representation? The situation in political parties is far from different – a worse situation obtains there. There is need for women's participation in the cause of the party, but they are unwelcome in their councils. The sooner the situation changes, the better it is for society as a whole. Ill educated, backward women are a menace to the society, state and even to men. Usually, when neglected and ignored, they demand for authoritarianism and tyranny. Let men beware and bestir themselves. Reservation of at least 30 per cent of seats in the legislative bodies, from the *panchayat* to parliament, for women will go a long way towards saving the situation.

The rights of women which are to be promoted and protected are neither high pitched nor unreasonable. It is for the reasonable and enlightened men to see the justness of the women's cause and support it. Many an enlightened man has supported, nay, fought for women's progress in the past, i.e., in the pre-independence period, especially in the nineteenth century. Why should men of the present times feel shy to support woman's cause, if not champion it? Any how, it is for women to take a stand for themselves and fight for their dignity and just rights. They may take the aid and assistance of progressive men but let it not be forgotten that they have to rely to themselves. It is sad, but true fact that women, who constitute one-half of humanity, have always been treated as second-class citizens and denied even basic rights, in most cases. Though 1975 was observed as the international women's year, 1975-85 as the International women's decade and March 8 as the International Women's Day each year, precious little seems to have been done to the protection and promotion of the rights of women in general. Recently many measures have been undertaken for the protection of women's rights. The committee on the status of women (1974) provided the first comprehensive study on the rights and status of Indian women. Recently, the Department of Women and Child Development has drawn up a National Perspective Plan for Women (1988-2000). 'Women's Studies' as a discipline is being encouraged in many universities, as well as by the UGC. Several pro-women laws have been passed, to protect their rights. However, these do not seem to be enough. Several concrete suggestions can be made for improving the lot of women in India.

Women should be given education. Education will broaden their outlook and make them aware of protecting their rights, duties and responsibilities in the society. Women should be encouraged to go in for higher education. Women should be encouraged to participate in politics. There should be reservation of seats for women both in the State Assemblies as well as in Parliament. Women should independently join politics, so that they can have a voice in nation building and can help the cause of women in general. A country which was ruled by a powerful woman Prime Minister, who was also a world stateswoman (Indira Gandhi), should boast of several women in its political sphere, who have an effective voice at all policy making levels.

Women should work as equal partners with men in all spheres of life. They should help build up a progressive and developed society. Women who work outside their homes are common today. In a country, where women are put on a pedestal and worshipped as Mother Goddess, crimes against women seem to be on the rise. The evil institution of dowry has led thousands of innocent young lives going up in flames. Recently several Acts and Bills have been passed to safeguard women, such as Dowry Prohibition Act, the Suppression of Immoral Traffic Act etc. After the passing of such Bills and Acts, an Indian woman feels safe and protected by law. More such acts should be passed, and possible loopholes should be blocked as these have far-reaching implications for women in the country.

Women should be given a special role in our planning process, and in the mobilization of local skills and resources. They should be brought into the mainstream of national development not as beneficiaries but as contributors and partakers along with men, and as rightful claimants of social security.

Women workers should be given more facilities. The existing laws should be made more stringent. Other suggestions for women industrial workers are provisions of crèches, adequate conservancy facilities, proper first aid and medical care facilities as well as vigilance to prevent exploitation by male workers. There is also a 'male-bias' in most industries and offices with regard to promotion and women complain of being 'sidetracked'. This should be avoided, and merit should be taken into account, both for appointment as well as for promotion. Male prejudices that label women as unreliable, soft, unsuitable for jobs and prone to absenteeism, should be done away with.

Women should realize that female infanticide and amniocentesis resulting in abortion of female fetuses should not be resorted to. The 'craze' for a son should be avoided, and a son and a daughter should be looked upon, treated and educated equally. Problems of gender bias and gender asymmetry should be tackled on a war footing.

Another suggestion for promoting and protecting the rights of women is to encourage the growth of more women's organizations in the country. The All India Women's Conference (AIWC) is the oldest women's organization in India. Also discussion should be held to make the public aware of women's issues. Eminent women should be invited to participate in and speak at these functions and exchange of views should be encouraged. The press and media should also give more attention to women's causes. Women's organizations should be like a pyramid, and should begin at the grassroots level and proceed to the top.

Above all, in order to protect women's rights, women have to become aware of their position as slaves. Unless she realizes that she is in bonds, she cannot aspire for freedom. Therefore, awareness of their miserable condition is a sine qua non for their liberation. They will have to get rid of their mental slavery. They should get rid of the feeling of inferiority to men. They will have to cultivate a scientific outlook coupled with a spirit of modernism and develop a rational frame of mind. When once they begin to question age old beliefs and time-worn ideas, then solutions will appear on their mental horizon. Thought leads to action. Perseverance and continuity of effort, together with intensity of struggle, will pave the way. In the beginning they may have to rely upon themselves. Later, as time progresses, enlightened men if not liberated men, i.e., liberated from feelings of superiority and male chauvinism, will also join the struggle. This will become a mighty force and the bastion of male dominated and exploitative society will collapse before the forces of women's progress and freedom

REFERENCES

1. The general function of law is to influence the subgroups and persons belonging to a society to conform to the group's expectation. Thus legislation is a means of social control.
2. In India customs or the way of life of the group is a very important binding force. Any deviation from customs provokes the wrath of the group. The essentials of a valid custom have been laid down by various courts in India and have been incorporated in the Hindu Marriage Act of 1955.
3. For instance, if institutionalization is successful, it facilitates the internalization of the new value by bringing about a change in the attitude and beliefs of the individual through social upbringing in the families. If such internalization does not take place, then the mere codification and the institutionalization will not have any social value. On the other hand, it may bring law itself into contempt. People may lose respect for law.
4. But there were informal social taboos against a man marrying a second wife when the first wife was alive. In the case of a second marriage he had to seek permission from his wife as well as from his relatives, which normally one never got except if the first wife was a chronic or was childless or gave birth only to a daughter. In other words, though law permitted them to marry, the involved social customs were against such marriage. For long, social reformers urged that Hindu marriage should be monogamous. Hindu women also have resented a second marriage by a man when his first wife is alive. This became more intense with increasing consciousness among women. Through participation in the freedom struggle they realized that the law does not provide

for equality between the sexes. Educated women fought this sexual discrimination. Orthodox Hindus opposed this because monogamy entails divorce and facilitates the remarriage of a divorced woman. They also feared that their whole social fabric would be affected by this change in law. This section was conscious too that polygamy meant discrimination against women. Finally after the enactment of Hindu Code Bill opposition gradually went down. Probably it is only in the remote villages that the new law may be violated out of ignorance. Thus this is a case where the social norms changed ahead of legal provisions.

5. For details, see M. C. Setalvad, *Law and Culture* (Allahabad: Chaitanya, 1965); *Social Welfare in India* (New Delhi: Government of India, 1960); K. M. Panikkar, *Hindu Society at Cross Roads* (Bombay: Asia Publishing House, 1961)
6. See Rama Mehta, "From Purdah to Modernity" in *Indian Women from Purdah to Modernity*, B. R. Nanda, ed., pp.113-128. See also M. N. Srinivas, *Ibid.*, pp.11-12, Tara Ali Baig, *India's Women Power* (New Delhi: 1976), p.212
7. CAI (LD), Official Report (23-25 February, 1949), Forth Session of the Constituent Assembly of India (1-23 February 1949) pp.419-28
8. *Ibid.*, p.420-21
9. CAI (LD), Vol.1, Part II, pp.426-27
10. For bias against inter-caste marriage also see Inderjeet Kaur, *Status of Hindu Women in India* (Allahabad: Chugh Publications, 1983) p.100
11. *The Tribune*, 6 November 1977
12. *The All India Reporter*, 1971, Vol. 58, pp.47-48
13. For details on dowry, see V.V. Prakasa Rao and V. Nandini Rao, Marriage, *The Family and Women in India* (New Delhi: Heritage, 1982) pp.61-105; L. Dumont, "Dowry in Hindu Marriage," *The Economic and Political Weekly*, XI (11 April 1959) pp.519-20; A.R. Gupta, *Women in Hindu Society* (New Delhi: Jyotsna Prakashan, 1976) pp.248-255; M.N. Srinivas, "Some Reflections on Dowry," J.P. Naik Memorial Lecture, 1983, Published for the Centre for Women's Development Studies, New Delhi, 1984
14. See Devaki Jain, "Indian Women: Today and Tomorrow," *The Hindustan Times*, 18 September 1983

15. See Promilla Kapur, *Marriage and Working Women in India* (Delhi: Vikas); S.C. Dube, "Men's and Women's Role in India: A Sociological Review," *Women in the New Asia*, Barbara E. Ward, ed.
16. M.S. Shah, "Wages and Employment of Women in India," *Indian Labour Journal*, Vol.XVII, No.2 (February 1975)
17. *Ibid.*
18. "Women in Industry," *Indian Labour Journal*, Vol. XVI, No.8 (August, 1975)

7
Conclusion

In the foregoing analysis, I have tried to look at issues pertaining to the rights of women from a purely conceptual point of view, that is, philosophically. In the first place, I strongly believe in the value of such an attempt because of the fact that 'ideology', to a very great extent, determines historical events and actions and attitudes of social groups, not to speak of individuals. The great ideology of liberty and equality won freedom for the French from tyrannical monarchies; the ideology of people's rule and their rights won American independence from imperialist Britain; nearer home, the exalted ideology of self-rule and non-violent protest brought independence to India. There have also been negative ideologies in history; the Nazi Holocaust was planned and executed upon the ideology that the German society made up of the supposedly superior Aryan race, should be based on likeness and exclusivity; Britain's colonial empire was motivated at least in part by the ideology that it was the 'white man's burden' to civilize 'backward' people. A very deep-rooted and central ideology has been the core of patriarchy as well; however, these ideologies, to a large extent, were responsible for the stereotypical and inhuman image of women wrought around oppressive structures and subsidiary ideologies and values of cultures and communities. Hence, a conceptual study on Indian women's rights from a feminist perspective is a valuable attempt in as much as it brings to light not only the 'ideology' behind oppressive structures in this country but also the 'ideology' which is an elaborate conceptual framework behind the main argument of the study, that is, the need for gender equality and equity within our still traditional, though changing, national situation. I believe that human beings can accept domination and inequality or freedom and equality only if they believe in the rightness or wrongness of power and authority. Ideology has an important role in maintaining the relations of power and domination which characterize gender relations in any society. Just as this ideology is the critical factor in maintaining gender inequality and gender injustice, the breaking of this difficult conceptual framework is the critical factor in heralding gender equality and justice. My work is an attempt in this direction.

I have approached the problem from a 'feminist perspective'; that is, the post-modern gender perspective which supercedes and positively remedies the traditional patriarchal perspective. It recognizes the equality of the sexes in the social roles they play. It also recognizes their differences in the biological roles. It also gives women much consideration for their contribution to the propagation of the human species. I have adopted a feminist stand without trying to be apologetic about being radical or extremist or anti-masculine. This I have done because of two reasons: (i) Layers of gender disparity have been accumulated over the years in most societies and these are still very deeply internalized and emotionally rooted in the Indian society, since the women's movement here began not so long ago. (ii) Women, in fact, are the central players in two very significant human activities of production and reproduction, that is, economic activity and the care of human beings, economic growth and human development. They also are the most responsible, and therefore with most at stake when the two realms work at cross purposes. Most importantly, they are the most sensitive to the need for better integration between the two realms mentioned, and hence their perspective is the most valid perspective for both economic growth and human development. It may be debated whether the above two conclusions are themselves deductions from the radical feminist perspective. However, I have arrived at the feminist perspective the other way round – that is, from a practical experience of the above two realizations. The feminist perspective that I have adopted here is thus both experiential and reflective. I need not add here that my own 'femininity' and its varied experiences, expressions and encounters were the strongest foundation for the perspective I have taken in this book. While to this extent there is a subjective air in the analysis and conclusions, when they are projected on the larger social context, one can clearly see how objectively certain they are. And I attribute the validity of the feminist perspective to this 'universalizable' characteristic of the feminist encounter itself to almost all contexts of cultures, languages, religions, communities, social stratifications, social roles and political ideologies up to about the middle of the 18th century (when the feminist ideology slowly, very slowly in fact, began to penetrate first the ideological framework).

After examining and analyzing the issues pertaining to the rights of women, I have reached to the conclusion that rights comprehend the whole of the conditions under which the voluntary actions of any person can be harmonized in reality with the voluntary action of every other person, according to the universal law of freedom. I have argued that rights and duties correlate in the context of men and women because they are capable of recognizing autonomy in others and participating in the moral community. The notion of women's rights involves in it the notion of power, privileges and claims. At the same time it also implies duty on others to recognize and respect women's rights. To recognize and respect women's rights not only means to refrain from interfering with the free exercise of their rights but also to assist women in attaining their rights.

I have also argued that there are certain fundamental human rights such as right to liberty, right to equality, right to dignity, right to life, right to fulfill one's needs and aspirations which are claimed equally by both men and women. There are also certain specific rights such as right to abortion and right to birth control which are specific and exclusively women's rights. Both women human generic rights and women gender specific rights nonetheless fall under the banner of human rights. All women's rights are human rights but all human rights are not women's rights since they are men's rights as well.

I have shown that violations against women in both private and public realms have to be brought to the light. In order to ensure the visibility of women's presence in the public sphere, women's dignity and security which are largely violated in the private space of the family and personal relationships are to be recognized and dealt with as human rights. This means that violence meted out by a traditional Indian mother-in-law to her daughter-in-law is an aspect of human rights violation just as it is a violation of women's rights. The recognition of women's rights as human rights makes it necessary to dismantle all the institutions and structures that oppress her and to set up systems and mechanisms to redress violations of gender justice. This recognition implies articulating and anlysing the violence that women face continuously. Violence against women is a critical tool in maintaining the relation of domination and subordination between men and women. It is all the more difficult to address because it is structurally integrated into most of the institutions of society. And while direct violence is visible and identifiable, the structural violence that women confront on a daily level is difficult to perceive without training and commitment. The commitment to address gender violence means recognizing and acknowledging the universality and indivisibility of human rights. Also, gender cuts across all sectors of the society. It is not a category to be confined to looking at the household but should provide an overarching perspective on all sectors. Whether it is environment, poverty, health, human rights or education, gender is of structural significance in each sector. And as we sharpen our understanding of the social construction of gender we begin to see how it provides a lens to look at a whole spectrum of issues. The tragedy in the Indian cultural scenario is that not to say of men even women themselves violate women's rights. Women's violence against women is as much morally blame-worthy as men's violence against women.

In India, our Constitution provides to all its citizens equality of status and of opportunity as well as justice – social, economic and political. Discrimination on the ground of sex has been abolished and women belonging to different religions and races have the same status before the law. However, law is a 'dumb' thing. It is accessible only to those who seek it, and even to those who seek it, law is sometimes 'blind'. Often law is not faithful to the realities of life; it rather follows the logic of proofs. In India many people still choose not to seek the law for lack of awareness and for lack of resources, monetary or otherwise. The law, despite being to a very great extent sufficient for improving the Indian women's plight revolutionarily, it is, in many respects, almost totally unable to change the social reality, the purpose for which they were created. This social reality is an intricate network of deeply ingrained beliefs and customs manifest in various subtle and evident aspects of rural life in this vast country. The law is inaccessible to these areas and to people who need them most. Protective discrimination in favour women is too insignificant in India. However, as per our national experience, this was one of the most successful experiments that paved the way of social change in favour of the scheduled castes and tribes. This needs to be encouraged in case of women as well. This is but a heatedly debated point, which cannot be given its due in a democratic debate because when it comes to a vote from the majority, women are often at the losing end since the masculine agenda will find the numbers in any male-dominated structure which obviously our democratic structure presently is. Hence, protective discrimination in case of women has to be debated scientifically, ideologically and in intellectual forums, before it finally comes to the portals of the citadel of democracy. The most recent example of how women's political struggles have found a hearing among men is the debate on the women's reservation bill in parliament. The fiercest opposition to this issue came from states like Uttar Pradesh and Bihar which have sent to the parliament some of its members who are not well educated and informed. Women's issues are still projected in our country as sophisticated urban jargon, which has no support from the rural majority. This in itself is a carefully knit political myth which needs to busted early. I have not argued that such discriminatory policy is the only way women's liberation in our country and legal battles cannot be fought here. What I have argued is that unless accessibility to legal procedures and legal literacy among the masses are drastically improved, the legal door to women's emancipation in India is not possible in the near future. If ingenious and innovative measures are planned for improving legal awareness and accessibility to law, things can change drastically. But this, by any count, has to be a gradual and tiresome process. Whereas protective discrimination, despite being a cruel joke on the oppressors of yore, becomes a reality almost immediately. The protection of women's rights does not victimize men. Giving some preferential treatment to women does not involve encroachment of men's rights to justice because it is intended only to equalize the playing field of opportunities for both men and women in the social context. It is not intended to bestow some benefits to one clan against another. To level the playing field for both men and women which is presently marked by inequalities is only to ensure equality of opportunity for both men and women within a society and to do this is not to do injustice against men because it is morally justified.

Though feminism and feminist movement is concerned with issues pertaining to the rights of women, feminism is not against men. This is not an apologetic statement to appease men or to gain their good will. It has a deeper foundation. Experiences of men and women everywhere, in all circumstances and contexts, when they are considered generically, show that women naturally tend to care, love and nurture much more than men can do. To say this does not mean that women should organize themselves into a movement to 'hate' men. It means only that men and women do differ in certain respects. In fact, women very often get into what is called the 'compassion trap' which is exclusive to women who feel that they exist to serve others, and who believe that they must provide tenderness and compassion to all at all times. The totally compassionate woman benefited society by making things more comfortable for men, so that men could tend to the 'more important concerns' of work, business, science, politics etc. Women today though go out of their homes, they still fall victim to the compassion trap and tend to go more for the helping professions like social work, nursing, teaching, domestic services etc. The compassion trap dictates that women express themselves by meeting the needs of others and by forgoing theirs in the meantime. Feminism asks women to get out of the compassion trap. Just as women are found to be the biggest contributors to grassroots level development in the Third World on account of the 'concern' they have for the welfare of their community, under the band of feminism women have come together as a movement to stand against all oppressive structures, hierarchies inside or outside the family, patriarchy, capitalism, imperialism, socialist dictatorships, religious fundamentalists, dominating husbands and the like. Feminism is also against women who become oppressive and dominating; it is against the oppression, domination and exploitation of any form by any men or women. I am of the opinion that men can also be feminists if they cultivate the typically feminine qualities and women can also be patriarchal if they choose to cultivate what is called the 'machismo' brand of masculinity. Biology does not determine one's ideology and beliefs. It is one's vision of the reality that determines one's ideology and beliefs. Feminism is a growing ideology. It is adhered to by all those who strongly believe in it. The nature and content of feminism is determined in each region according to the local situation, according to the perceptions and aspirations of the local women. Feminism is morally a justified challenging doctrine. It questions the network of all human social relationships marked by inequalities.

This special nature of women is not, however, a biological consequent of women's physique; in fact, individuals develop their nature while encountering the phenomenon of existence. All the plants and animals that share this planet with us have biologically-given natures and destinies. Each of them will follow the pattern appropriate for its species, live out its natural life-span, and become humus in the earth. Of all life on this planet, only we humans have the capacity to shape our lives around our own purposes. In fact, we need not even repeat the models of life-purposes our cultures dictate to us. We can choose independent purposes of our own, provided that they do not harm the purposes and lives of other humans who live with us. Hence, I here have taken an existentialist stance with the purpose of busting the myth that women have a specifically given 'feminine' nature, according to which are the atrocities heaped upon them. I believe that if women have to break free of the present impasse about the conceptual moorings of feminism itself, they should take an existentialist stance. The special 'nature' of women I here refer to is a product of the particular feminine experience in history on account of the particular roles they have played in the present society. Women have thus created a nature for themselves to be concerned and involved with basic needs, with the perpetuation of life, with keeping people alive, with preserving life – this is why women have to be central to development. This is another important argument of this book.

One of the most basic human needs is the desire for a sense of their own dignity, a need to be treated fully and completely human. I rate this need even a more basic 'human' need than the need for a food, shelter and clothing. While we are one with the animal kingdom in many of our basic needs, our need for dignity is uniquely human. This need for dignity is rooted in our need for freedom and liberty, fair treatment, equality before the law, the demand that one is not penalized simply because of one's race, religion or sex and that no group be branded as inferior by being forcibly subjected to another, whether it be on the ground of race or religion or sex. Rousseau is wrong when he said that women have the same desires as men, but do not have the same right to express them. But when this question is asked: why do women have no right to express themselves and their desires? no reasonable answer is found. The only answer which is given is that men have dictated gender equations so far. This is not a reasonable answer at all. Hence there is a need to change it since it is men's unjustified construction. Kant was absolutely right when he said: "Act in such a way that you always treat humanity, whether in your own person or in the person of any other, never simply as a means, but always at the same time as an end." Men and women should be treated equally without any discrimination and if they are treated different, it must be done on a morally justified ground and not arbitrarily. The social reality today is that people are not treated as an end in themselves. They are treated as means. This is true not only of developing countries like India, but of developed countries as well. Women want that they should be treated as human beings and not as things or properties, bereft of dignity and freedom.

I have argued in the various chapters above that Hindu social norms based on religious dogmas and premises were anti-women. Hindu social norms do not preserve women's freedom and dignity of living barring few cases. I have shown that the later onslaught against women was a definite and purposeful masculine agenda which unfortunately came in the sacrosanct religious garb, difficult to be broken due to the Eastern mental framework of not compartmentalizing the religious stratum from the non-religious social stratum. I have argued strongly against the *Manusmriti*'s picture of woman. I have talked about the Muslim personal law and the Christian tradition of patriarchy, although my point of emphasis was the Hindu social and ethical code. In fact all the religions in the history of humankind meted out a raw deal to women. Manu pictures women to be subject to her father in childhood, to her husband when married and to her sons when widowed. Chanakya prescribes that women should purify herself of her sins by drinking the water in which her husband's feet had been washed. Buddha, despite being a social reformer of his times, advised Ananda never to look at a woman lest she entice him. The *Vinaya Pitaka* categorically stated that a woman can never attain *nirvana*. The *Koran* prescribes its adherents that while dividing the inheritance give to a male one portion equal to that of two females and if a woman was guilty of impurity she had to be confined until death after taking the witness of four persons. Islamic law also allows a man to keep up to four wives. The

Bible prescribes that women should be subject to their husbands and men should look after them as they would a weak vessel. Several Biblical proverbs paint women as freakish, quarrelsome and unwise. I have argued strongly against all such religiously wrought social stigma against women as well as social norms against women that have a religious backing. I am of the opinion that unless religious and cultural structure of our society is changed, there is no hope for a better future for women. Religious norms and rationales are changeable as they are 'man-made' and not as the propagandists would like us to believe, 'inspired' or given from above. If any of the scriptural and sacred teachings are 'given', 'inspired' or 'heard', these could only be the spiritual message and not the social norms, which are always reflective of the prevalent equations of the power structures of one group upon another and one individual to another.

There is a prevalent trend among intellectuals to speak of our glorious cultural and religious traditions of treating women like goddesses by quoting examples of goddess-worship. But unfortunately this mythological existence remains only in temples and scriptures and in intellectual discussions on culture. Ironically, there are temples of the Mother Goddess where women are not only not allowed to enter but also disallowed to partake of its *prasad*. What are prevalent in society are by and large all negative views about a woman. This system of looking upwards, forwards and towards a man in ideological, social, political, economic, legal and other realms for tutelage is what patriarchy denotes. It is a great superstructure of women's oppression. Religion and its symbols are not the only patriarchal realms in this country. Family, politics, media, entertainment, sports, cultural pursuits, employment, academics, education – all that is worthy of the human interest is largely reserved for men through the unwritten laws of patriarchy. It raises doubts if democracy can function in a country where people are tradition-ridden, ignorant and callous about their own basic rights. Only when women are given their rightful place and their due can Indian democracy, the biggest democratic institution on Planet Earth as we boast, can have any meaning.

I have not only argued in the book for the equality of women from a feminist perspective. While this is the ideal reform that women in India should ultimately aim for, I have shown through analysis that a lesser immediate goal would be the emancipation of women in some particular ways, like removal of oppressive patriarchal power structures and symbols through law (which is being done with some quickness and focus already) and through enlightenment of the minds of women and men. The long-term goal of social transformation that ensures women's right and their liberation from exploitation, subjugation, superstition, degradation and injustice can be achieved only through these smaller battles. Of course, most battles are won in the mind first. The feminist battle would primarily be won in the minds of women first and then in the minds of men. Women bear the triple burden of job, housework and children because, first of all, they are willing to wear the mantle of this three-fold responsibility due to their cultural conditioning, and secondly because men want this type of a social order to continue for their own advantages and comforts. The reality that woman reproduce, conceive and bear children seems to be the primary reason to rationalize her confinement to a purely reproductive role, a role around which the oppressive natural, metaphoric, cultural and religious language against woman is woven. This is used as an easy tool to diffuse discussions on women's rights and justice immediately on the ground of fear of being unnatural and destructive of humanity and civilization. Woman's oppression and subordination is so deeply wrought into her biology that redemption appears to her as going against her own nature. But in fact 'praxis' or conscious purposeful activity is what distinguishes humans from nature and so it is possible for woman to view her reproductive role as 'praxis' and not as biological destiny. From time immemorial women have consciously performed the reproductive role and have found ways to prevent the reproductive cycle within her. This shows the feasibility of viewing reproduction as a practical role rather than women's nature. However, the intellectual obstacle still persists in seeing reproduction as a conscious human choice and activity. The physical birth seems to obscure the human choice involved. For this to happen we need to open up institutions like family, motherhood and marriage, all spheres of human activity like beliefs and cultural practices, structure of labour, power and sexuality, decision making to questioning. We need to differentiate the socially constructed elements from the biologically given so that more vistas for change are opened up. The emancipation of women is handicapped by a number of causes like their passive role, social ills, omestic compulsions, illiteracy, wrong perceptions, ignorance and superstitions. Layers and layers of poor self-image and submissive frameworks are heavily weighing our women down. These have to be washed away through women's liberation ideology and actual movements. Further, woman's emancipation depends not only on this intellectual revolution but also on the functional prerequisite of self-reliance and economic independence. Women need encouragement to develop self-confidence and skills which will make them economically self-reliant, which can be achieved through the focus given in the whole process of education.

I have tried to maintain throughout this book a holistic and inclusive campaign in favour of women's rights than a divisive, one-sided and exclusivist campaign. That is, I have not argued that women's issues are affecting women only and that they have to be fought and won by women only. Such a position is, however, not uncommon among radical feminists, especially in the West. They have sometimes gone to the extent of saying that women should stay separately in this oppressive society, marriage as an institution of oppression should be abolished and the oppressive structures created through social contract should be violently opposed. I have not taken this type of position, although my perspective is nevertheless wholly feminist. I have argued that issues pertaining to women's rights do not concern women alone. They are concerns of the society. Women's demand is not for equality in every respect with men within the given social system. Women's demand is for equality in the relevant respects. Their demand is for a new society based on harmonious relationship between men and women. There is no doubt about it that men and women differ physically, and psychologically in many respects. But this does not mean that they share no commonality. Equality in every respect may not be socially desirable nor may it be possible, given their specific nature. But equality of consideration and equality of opportunity in equal field and in equally morally relevant respect is desirable for the development of individuals and society at large.

In any of the chapters above I have not dealt one very important point in connection with the gender movement due to certain limitations but one thing I would like to mention very briefly here. This is about the 'ethics' of speaking on women's issues. Women all over the world feel gravely guilty about their being assertive for the feminist causes. Some 'masculinists', if one may call them so, have argued that this 'guilt' is a primordial emotion which goes to show that women's present status is dictated by the natural order and nothing should be done to change it except to humanity's own peril. But then question is: Is this 'masculinist' claim justified? Is this 'feminist guilt' justified or is it primordial? Is it ethical to be 'feminist'? These are some of the issues which need further investigation. One thing seems to be quite obvious that in order to answer these questions broadly, one only needs to think of the atrocities and violence heaped upon women throughout the centuries. There need not be any debate on the absolutely unjustified position on the issues of violence against women. If these are justified, violence and injustice against people on the basis of race, religion or language also will have to be accepted. But such things cannot be accepted since they rest on irrationality. In fact, our national justification for protective discrimination in favour of the scheduled castes and tribes is the centuries of oppression we as a nation heaped on these sections of our population. Today these issues have been politicized and the review of protective discrimination has virtually become impossible, although the framers of our constitution formulated this policy only as a provisional arrangement for ensuring social justice for all sections of our population equally. Similarly, past injustice against women, probably much more grotesque and wide-spread than all other forms of injustice in our society, is enough justification today for the feminist agenda that may be designed at any level in our country, whether political, bureaucratic, social, religious or whatever. We have to change the cultural structures that we have in our society which perpetrate gender imbalances and gender violence. Women feel guilty about questioning these issues. Unless we bring changes in social structures, the platform and mechanism for ensuring women's rights are not readily at hand. If this is not done, we cannot stop gender violence; we cannot hope for the betterment of women's life. Hence this is the practical necessity for disturbing the social structures based on discrimination. Feminists need not feel guilty about championing women's cause. If they feel guilty they only need to remember the old saying of the great *Talmund*: 'If I am not for myself, who will be for me? If I am not for others, who am I for? And if not now, when?' If one does not stand up for one's own honour, people will assume that she had no honour. All structures and forms of gender imbalance should be changed from within and the 'feminine mystique' perpetuated by consumerism, the media and other institutions should be effectively resisted. Gender cleansing the educational language is the most important means to gender equity. We become what we are taught in our childhood. Although we continuously learn and change and improve as dynamic beings, we are also stifled (or opened up positively as the case may be) in our growth by our education, upbringing and training, especially of our childhood. Hence, parental education and structured education should both be gender-neutral. While informal parental education cannot be tailored so much by public policy and thus cannot be monitored that well, formal education can be changed through policy making. This latter step has to be taken up urgently to make our society gender balanced. The feminist cause, I believe, is a giant step towards personal freedom and growth for both women and men.

Bibliography

Besides the following books and articles, I have also relied heavily on the Indian classics like *the Vedas, the Bhagavatgita, the Mahabharata, the Ramayana, Manusmriti, Arthasastra* etc.

A. Books

Agnew, Vijay, *Elite Women in Indian Politics* (New Delhi: Vikas Publishing House, 1979)

Akerkar, Supriya, "Theory and Practice of Women's Movement in India," *Economic and Political Weekly*, Vol.XXX, No.17

Altekar, A.S., *The Position of Women in Hindu Civilization* (Delhi: Motilal Banarsidass, 2nd Edn., 1983)

Arthur, E. Morgan, *A Search for Purpose* (Ahmedabd: Jivanji Dahyab Desai, 1957)

Baig, Tara Ali, *India's Women Power* (New Delhi: n.p., 1976)

Baily, S.G., *Comparative Political System Studies in the Politics of Pre-Industrial Societies*, ed., Ronald Cohen and John Middleton (New York: n.p.,1963)

Banthiya, Ruchi, *From Historicity to Postmodernity* (Jaipur: Rawal, 1994)

Barlin, Isaiah, *Four Essays on Freedom* (London: Oxford University Press, 1969)7

Barrett, Michele, *Women's Oppression Today* (London: Verso, 1980)

Bushky, Henry Jeffreys, *Widow Burning: A Narrative* (London: Longmen, 1955)

CAI (LD), Official Report (23-25 February, 1949), *Forth Session of the Constituent Assembly of India* (1-23 February 1949)

Compbell, A.H., *Obligation and Obedience to Law* (New York: Oxford University Press, 1965)

Compbell, C.H., *The Philosophical Concept of Man* (Moscow: Progress Publishers, 1988)

Cormack, M., *She Who Rides a Peacock : Indian Students and Social Change* (Bombay: Asia Publishing House, 1961)

Cranston, Maurice William, *What are Human Rights?* (New York: 1963)

Desai, Neera and Krishmaraj, Maithreyi, *Women and Society in India* (Delhi: Ajanta Publications, 1987)

Document of the Fourth UN World Conference on Women

Everett, J. M., *Women and Social Change in India* (New Delhi: Heritage Publishers, 1978)

Firestone, Schulasmith, *The Dialectic of Sex* (New York: Bantam Books, 1970)

Forsythe, David P., *Human Rights in World Politics* (London: University of Nebraska Press, 1983)

Freire, Paulo, *Pedagogy of the Oppressed*, trans., Myre Berguan Ramos (New York: Harder and Herder, 1970)

Gandhi, M.K., *Women and Social Inustice* (Ahmedabad: Navjivan Publishing House, 1942)

Gharpure, J.R., *Rights of Women under the Hindu Law* (Bombay: Bombay University, 1943)

Gill, K., *Hindu Women's Property in India* (New Delhi: Deep and Deep Publications, 1986)

Gorwaney, N., *Self Image and Social Change : A Study of Female Students* (New Delhi: Sterling Publishers, n.y)

Gupta, A.R., *Women in Hindu Society* (New Delhi: Jyotsna Prakashan, 1976)

Hate, Chandrakala, *Changing Status of Women* (Bombay: Allied Publishers, 1969)

Hobbes, Thomas, *Leviathan*, in Frederick A. Olafson, ed., *Society, Law, and Morality : Readings in Social Philosophy from Classical and Contemporary Sources* (New Jersey: Prentice-Hall, 1961)

Kant, Immanuel, *The Science of Right*, in Frederick A. Olafson, ed., *Society, Law, and Morality : Readings in Social Philosophy from Classical and Contemporary Sources* (New Jersey: Prentice-Hall, 1961)

Kapadia, K. M., *Marriage and Family in India* (Bombay: Oxford University Press, 1958)

Kapur, Promilla, *Marriage and Working Women in India* (Delhi: Vikas, n.y)

Kaur, Inderjeet, *Status of Hindu Women in India* (Allahabad: Chugh Publications, 1983)

Kaushik, Sushila, ed., *Women in Society: Women's Oppression and Perspective* (New Delhi: Vikas Publishing House, 1985)

Locke, John, *Second Treatise on Civil Government*, in Frederick A. Olafson, ed., *Society, Law, and Morality : Readings in Social Philosophy from Classical and Contemporary Sources* (New Jersey: Prentice-Hall, 1961)

Majumdar, P. N., *Races and Cultures of India* (New Delhi: Asia Publishing House, n.y)

Majumdar, Vina, ed., *Symbols of Power: Studies on the Political Status of Women in India* (Bombay: Allied Publishers, 1979)

Mehta, R., *The Western Educated Hindu Women* (Bombay: Asia Publishing House, 1970)

Meillassoux, Cloude, *Maidens, Meal and Money* (Cambridge: Cambridge University Press, 1981)

Nanda, B.R., *Indian Women from Purdah to Modernity* (New Delhi: Vikas Publishing House, 1976)

Pal, Radha Binod, *The History of Hindu Law* (Calcutta: University of Calcutta, 1958)

Panikkar, K. M., *Hindu Society at Cross Roads* (Bombay: Asia, 1961)

Prabhu, P., *Hindu Social Organisation* (Bombay: Popular Book Depot, 1958)

Prasad, Anirudh, *Social Engineering and Constitutional Protection of Weaker Sections in India* (New Delhi: Deep and Deep Publications, 1980)

Rao, V.V. Prakasa and Rao, V. Nandini, Marriage, *The Family and Women in India* (New Delhi: Heritage, 1982)

Rawls, J., *A Theory of Justice* (Oxford: Oxford Paperbacks, 1971)

Rousseau, Jean-Jacques, *A Discourse on the Origin of Inequality*, in Frederick A. Olafson, ed., *Society, Law, and Morality : Readings in Social Philosophy from Classical and Contemporary Sources* (New Jersey: Prentice-Hall, 1961)

Roy, Shibane, *Status of Muslim Women in North India* (Delhi: B.R. Publishing Company, 1979)

Setalvad, M. C., *Law and Culture* (Allahabad: Chaitanya, 1965)

Setalvad, M. C., *Social Welfare in India* (New Delhi: Government of India, 1960)

Shastri, Shakuntala Rao, *Women in the Vedic Age*, 3rd edn. (Bombay: Baratiya Vidya Bhavan, 1960)

Singh, Y.B., *Social Life in Ancient India* (New Delhi: Life and Light Publishers, 1981)

The UN World Conference on Women at Beijing; "Platform for Action"

Universal Declaration of Human Rights of the United Nations as adopted in 10 December 1948

Upadhyaya, B. S., *Women in Rigveda* (New Delhi: S. Chand and Co., 1974)

Venkatarayappa, *Feminine Roles* (Bombay: Popular Prakashan, 1966)

B. Articles

Acharjit, Nilima, "Women Workers in Organized and Unorganized Sectors in India," *Indian Worker*, Vol.29, No.23, March 1981

Aggarwal, R.C., "Proprietary Rights of Women," *Social Welfare*, Vol.20, No.4, July 1973

Ahuja, Ram, "Female Education in India," *Social Welfare*, Vol.20, No.19, Dec. 1973

Amma, P. Janaki, "Special Legislation for Protection of Women and children," *Cochin University Law Review*, Vol.5, No.1, March 1981

Anjaneyulu, Hemlate, "In Fulfillment of Her Destiny," *Swarajya*, Vol.23, No.51, 1979

Ayer, A. J., "Free Will and Necessity," *Free Will*, ed., Gary Watson (New York: Oxford University Press, 1982)

Ayer, A. J., "Free Will and Rationality," *Philosophical Subject*, ed., Zak Van Straatan (Oxford: Clarendon Press, 1980)

Baig, Tara Ali, "Crimes against Women Genesis," *Mainstream*, Vol.19, 1980

Balasubramanyam, Vimal, "Ads and Decent Wedding Cult," *Mainstream*, Vol.21, No.49, August 1983

Balasubramanyam, Vimal, "Dreaded Daughters," *Mainstream*, Vol.28, August 1982

Banerjee, M. N., "Hindu Family and Freudian Theory," *Indian Journal of Social Work*, 1944-45

Banerjee, Nirmala, "Women Workers and Development," *Social Scientist*, Vol.6, No.8, March 1978

Banerjee, Santosh Kumar, "Divorce in Hindu Marriage," *Population Review*, Vol.14, Nos.1-2, January

Basu, Jagiraj, "Education of Women in Vedic India," *Visvabharati Quarterly*, Vol.37, No.2, 1971-72

Bentinck, William, "On the Suppression of Sati," *Vivekananda Kendra Patrika*, Vol.5, No.2, August 1976

Berry, Ramesh, "Marxism and Women of the Vedic Age," *Socialist World*, April, 1975

Bhagyalakshmi, J., "Girl Child: Unwanted, Neglected and Suffering," *Kurukshetra*, Vol.38, No.12, 1990

Bhatnagar, Subir Kumar, "Special Provisions for Women: A Case of Judicial Ambivalence," *Law Journal of Guru Nanak Dev University*, Vol.X, No.2, June 1982

Bidara Koppa, G.S., "Position and Problems of Hindu Widows," *Journal of Karnataka University Social Sciences*, Vol.7, 1971

Blake, Ralph Mason, "On Natural Rights," *Readings in Ethical Theory*, Wilfrid Sellars and John Hospers, eds., Second Edition (New Jersey: Prentice-Hall, 1970)

Brown, Stuart M. Jr., "Inalienable Rights," *Philosophical Review*, Vol.64, No.2, 1955

Butalia, Bela, "Real Issues and Wrong Emphasis," *Mainstream*, Vol.21, August 1982

Byrnes, Andrew, "Women, Feminism and International Human Rights Law - Methodological Myopia, Fundamental Flaws or Meaningful Marginalisation?: Some Current Issues," in www.hrw.org quoted from *12th Australian Year Book of International Law*

Chandrakanthi, G., "Women in India: Past, Present and Future," *Swarajya*, Vol.19, No.22, Nov 1974

Chandrasekhar, S., "Indian Women: Myth and Reality," *Realist*, Jan 1968

Chatterjee, Kapila, "Dowry Custom: Barbarous and Anti-Hindu," *Vivekanand Kendra Patrika*, Vol.2, No.2, August 1973

Chattopadhyaya, Kamladevi, "Some Thought on Women's Education," *Indian Review*, Vol.68, No.3, 1972

Chaudhary, R., "Status and Role of Women : Great Indian Women through the Ages," *Role and Status of Women in Indian Society* (Calcutta: Firma KLM, 1978)

Chaudhary, R., "The Position of Women in Medieval India," *Modern Review*, Vol.93, No.6, 1953

Chitnis, Suma, "Women and Development," *The Indian Journal of Social Work*, Vol.XLIII, No.4, Jan 1983

Cosper, D. Dale, "Simone de Beauvoir," *Microsoft® Encarta® 98 Digital Encyclopedia*. © 1993-1997 Microsoft Corporation

Cruikshank, Barbara R., "Patriarchy," *Microsoft® Encarta® 98 Digital Encyclopedia*. © 1993-1997 Microsoft Corporation

Das, D.P., "Dowry and Social Change," *Weekly Round Table*, Vol.2, No.30, August 26, 1973

Das, Pushpa Lata, "Women Power," *Sarvodaya*, Vol.27, Nos.7-8, Jan-Feb 1978

Desai, Neera, "Social Movements: Struggle for Indian Women's Emancipation," *Indian Journal of Social Research*,Vol.29, 1988

Deshmukh, D., "New Dimensions of Women's Life in India," *Social Welfare*, Vol.3, No.9, Dec 1955

Deshpande, Anjali, "A New Menace," *Mainstream*, Vol.21, July 1982

Deshpande, Anjali, "A New Woman", *Mainstream*, Vol.21, No.20, Jan 1983

Dube, S.C., "Men's and Women's Role in India: A Sociological Review," *Women in the New Asia*, Barbara E. Ward, ed.

Dumont, L., "Dowry in Hindu Marriage," *The Economic and Political Weekly*, XI (11 April 1959)

Dutta, N.K., "Widow in Ancient India," *Indian Historical Quarterly*, Vol.14, No.4, Dec 1938

Farooqi, Vimla, "Crime against Women-struggle, *Mainstream*, Vol.19

Fonseca, M.B., "Family Disorganization and Divorce in Indian Community," *Sociological Bulletin*, Vol.12, No.2, Sept 1963

Ghotoskar, Siyata and Kanhere, Vijay, "The Role of Women in Social Change and People's Movements," *Social Action*, Vol.XXXIV, No.2, April-June 1984

Gould, Carol C., "Freedom and Women," *Journal of Social Philosophy*, Vol.XV, Nov 1984, Fall

Gupta, Balram, "Protective Discrimination in Favour of Women Under the Indian Constitution," *Law Journal of Guru Nanak Dev University,* Vol.X, No.2, June 1982

Hoksar, Nandita, "Sati and National Perspective, *Mainstream*, Vol.19, No.16, Dec 1980

Hoksar, Nandita, "Women's Problems: Three Approaches," *Mainstream*, Vol.20, Nos.1-5, September 1981

Jain, Devaki, "Indian Women: Today and Tomorrow," *The Hindustan Times*, 18 September 1983

Jena, Vandan Kumari, "Women and Development," *Indian Journal of Public Administration*, Vol.36, No.4, 1989

Lyle, Jerolyn Ross, "Civil and Political Rights for Minorities and Women in India," *Bulletin of the Ramakrishna Mission Institute of Culture*, Vol.30, No.6, June 1979

Mahajan, Amarjit, "Women's Two Roles: A Study of Role Conflict," *The Indian Journal of Social Work*, Vol.XXVI, No.4, Jan 1966

Mann, R.S., "Acculturation and Women's Standing," *The Indian Journal of Social Work*, Vol.XXII, No.2, Sept 1961

McCloskey, H. J., "Respect for Human Moral Rights versus Maximizing Good," *Utility and Rights*, R. G. Frey, ed. (Oxford: Basil Blackwell, 1985)

Mehta, Rama, "From Purdah to Modernity" in *Indian Women from Purdah to Modernity*, B. R. Nanda, ed.

Nath, Kamla, "Women in the Working Force in India," *Economic and Political Weekly*, Vol.III, No.31, Augu 1968

Nijjar, Bakha Shih Singh, "Women and Social Slavery in the Punjab," *Journal of Indian History*, Vol.56, No.3, Dec 1978

Patel, Ahooja Krishna, "Profile of a Battered Indian Woman," *Mainstream*, Vol.18, No.27, March 1979

Remanamma, A and Bambawle, Usha, "Transitory Status Images of Working Women in Modern India," *the Indian Journal of Social Work*, Vol.XLV, No.2, July 1984

Shah, M.S., "Wages and Employment of Women in India," *Indian Labour Journal*, Vol.XVII, No.2 (February 1975)

Singh, Khushpal, "Women – Their Status, Role and the Law," *Law Journal of Guru Nanak Dev University*, Vol.X, No.3-4, Sept-Dec 1982

Srinivas, M.N., "Some Reflections on Dowry," J.P. Naik Memorial Lecture, 1983, Published for the Centre for Women's Development Studies, New Delhi, 1984

Sudha, G., "Changing Status of Women in Society," *Women: Her Problems and Her Achievements*, ed., Sarojni Shintri, (Dharwad: Karnatak University, 1977)

Taganmohan, Rao R., "Dowry System in India: A Socio-legal Approach to the Problem," *Journal of Indian Law Institute*, Vol.15, No.4, Octo-Dec 1993

Thlhami, Ghada, "The Human Rights of Women in Islam," *Journal of Social Philosophy*, Vol.XVI, No.1, Winter, 1985

Varandani, Gursharan, "Legal Protection to Women Workers in India – A Critical Appraisal," *Law Journal of Guru Nanak Dev University*, Vol.X, No.2, June 1982

Index